ARCHITECTURAL DELINEATION

A Photographic Approach to Presentation

ERNEST BURDEN

2d Edition

Library of Congress Cataloging in Publication Data

Burden, Ernest E., date.
  Architectural delineation.

  Includes index.
  1. Architectural rendering.   I. Title.
NA2780.B87   1981   720'.28'4   81-15631
ISBN 0-07-008925-6   AACR2

1234567890   HDHD   898765432

ISBN 0-07-008925-6

The editors for this book were Joan Zseleczky and Christine M. Ulwick,
the designer was Ernest Burden, and the production supervisor
was Teresa F. Leaden. It was set in Folio by York Graphic Services.

Printed and bound by Halliday Lithograph.

CONTENTS

v

ABOUT THE AUTHOR

Ernest Burden studied at the Rhode Island School of Design and with pioneering architect Bruce Goff at the University of Oklahoma, where he earned his Bachelor of Architecture degree.

Currently active as a presentation consultant, he has developed a visual marketing slide/cassette program for use in training design professionals in presentation techniques. He is also publisher of a bimonthly newsletter, "The Presentation ADVISOR," which is directly related to presentation techniques.

Previous books he has authored on the subject of presentations include: *Visual Presentation—A Practical Manual for Architects and Engineers* (McGraw-Hill); *Visual Marketing* (Eastman Kodak); *Entourage: A Tracing File for Architecture and Interior Design Drawing* (McGraw-Hill) and the first edition of this book, *Architectural Delineation,* which sold over 30,000 copies.

ARCHITECTURAL DELINEATION

McGraw-Hill Book Company

New York   St. Louis   San Francisco
London   Madrid   Paris   Tokyo
Toronto   Mexico   Sydney

PREFACE

Are today's methods of delineation as up to date as the buildings they depict? Perhaps not, considering that a Renaissance artist would feel quite at home in today's studio or classroom. It was the Renaissance artist who witnessed the birth and development of the concept of perspective, a concept that had eluded everyone for centuries. This development of perspective happened simultaneously with the discovery and application of certain principles of optics that led to the earliest form of camera, the camera obscura.

Here for the first time one could trace a true-to-life image on the glass of the camera back. By the year 1685, the camera was completely ready and waiting for photography. However, its use and development were not realized for 200 years, until the development of sensitized paper. The camera obscura, though, remained the useful and popular tool of the artist for many years. Eventually, this simple device was replaced by an elaborate system of mathematical and geometrical constructions. This method, developed during the Renaissance, persists to this very day. Fortunately, through the development of its counterpart, the camera has taken greater strides in helping human beings to see and record the world they live in.

To "delineate" means to draw, trace, or outline a form, but, taken in its broadest sense, it means to depict accurately. It is this concept which must be restored to the field of presentation. The time-consuming, archaic methods of plotting perspectives have no place in our modern world. The alternative of approximated "eyeball" perspectives is not satisfactory to depict today's concepts of building design. What is truly needed is a quick, accurate, and flexible system, and here the camera provides a ready answer. The ideas and examples provided in this book will contribute toward restoring delineation to its proper perspective. Today's delineation can best be described as a drawing that is a precursor of a photograph of the completed project.

ACKNOWLEDGMENTS

Most architectural renderings precede the actual building by several years. Some projects may never become realities for one reason or another. Others may undergo such extensive revisions that the design, as originally conceived and rendered, may not resemble the finished product.

It is with this in mind that I thank all the architects listed in the "Design Credits" following the text for permission to publish the renderings of their projects. I extend these thanks equally to those architects who provided drawings of their projects done by other delineators. And I must express my gratitude to those delineators for their fine contribution to this book.

I appreciate the assistance given to me by those directly concerned with the production of this book, including those who helped make and remake the photographs.

Many thanks to my friends the editors at McGraw-Hill who have made the production of this book a valuable experience.

To my wife Karen, I owe much for her understanding and encouragement during the many years that encompassed the original production of this book and its subsequent revision.

Ernest Burden

Introduction

The first edition of this book introduced a new concept to the existing rendering layout techniques then in use. This new technique involved the use of the camera to replace the time-consuming mechanical methods. The book also illustrated many drawings and layout examples demonstrating the author's application and use of those techniques in his own practice.

Now, a decade later, the concepts behind those techniques are unchanged. Therefore, in considering material for the first major revision of this book, those items have remained an integral part of the new edition. Since the publication of the first edition, however, many new examples and applications have been produced. These new projects have all been selected to further demonstrate and enhance the basic photograph concept.

Many new drawings were provided by other professional delineators. Their work is shown under their own names rather than those of the projects in most cases. All work not directly credited to other delineators is the work of the author. Although the last professional drawing produced by the author was in 1975 (Westchester One, page 87), he is still active in other forms of presentation work. This mainly encompasses slide presentation and visual marketing techniques. Material in the first edition relating to slide presentations has been incorporated to produce a much more extensive book on presentation techniques.

While the basic concepts do not change in a decade, the style of architecture does, and so, too, do the various techniques used to depict these new styles. Therefore, nearly half this new edition is devoted to new work.

Many of the new drawings and projects came directly from the architect's own office and sometimes from the architect's own hand. Some of the larger firms now have a full-time delineator on staff. This provision demonstrates the importance of professional-quality work on presentation drawings. Drawings of these various projects are listed under the project name. Design credits for all the drawings in this book are listed on pages 274–278.

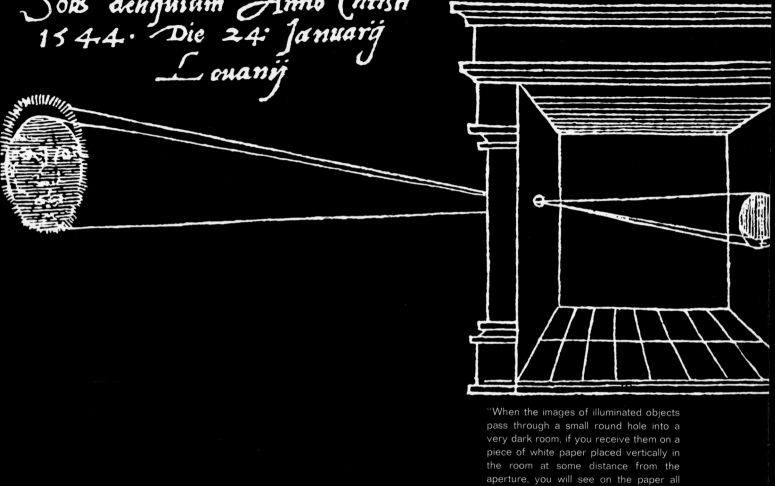

"When the images of illuminated objects pass through a small round hole into a very dark room, if you receive them on a piece of white paper placed vertically in the room at some distance from the aperture, you will see on the paper all these objects in their natural shapes and colors. They will be reduced in size and upside down, owing to the intersection of the rays at the aperture."

—The notebooks of
Leonardo da Vinci.

Camera Obscura

The invention of the camera obscura has been erroneously attributed to Alberti, Roger Bacon, and Leonardo da Vinci. It was, in fact, described by the Arabian scholar Alhazen before 1038, although knowledge of it can be traced back to Aristotle. The first published illustration of the camera obscura by a Dutch physician in 1544 described a method of observing solar eclipses. It was soon discovered that by this means one could see things going on in the street as well.

The camera obscura, in its original form, was the darkened room in a house. This is where the name originated, "camera obscura" meaning literally a dark room. The first significant improvement to it was the inclusion of a biconvex lens in the aperture to form a brighter image. The next improvement transformed the box-type camera into a reflex-type camera. A plane mirror at a 45-degree angle to the lens reflected the image the right way up onto a piece of oiled paper stretched across the opening in the top of the camera.

In 1685 the camera was ready for photography as we know it today. What was needed was a method by which the images produced by the camera obscura could be fixed. Louis J. M. Daguerre had for many years been trying to fix the images automatically instead of tracing them by hand. He used the camera obscura to achieve realistic detail and perfect perspective. He finally succeeded in developing a method of fixing the image on a polished silver plate. Details of the method known as daguerreotype were much publicized. No knowledge of drawing or manual dexterity was necessary. Anyone could succeed with the same certainty and perform as well as the author of the invention. This day, the nineteenth of August, 1839, stands as the official birthdate of photography. Many exclaimed in excitement, "From today painting is dead!"

1

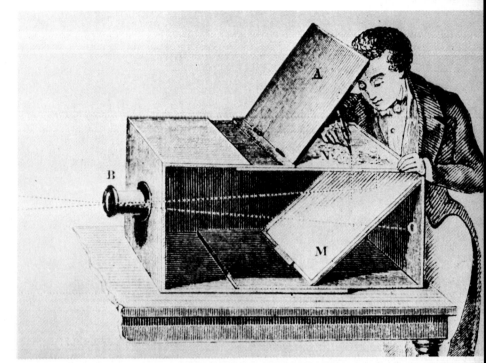

2

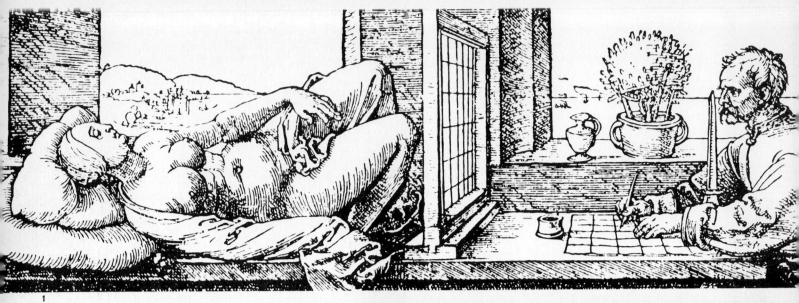

1

A Comparison of Systems

Vision is a process whereby light rays, reflected from objects outside, are received by the eye's lens. This lens condenses the rays to a point, from which the rays reemerge to focus a small, inverted image on the retina, a wall of light-sensitive cells. The retina transmits the light messages across the optic nerve to the brain, which comprehends these messages as a picture of the object. The brain automatically turns the image right side up and laterally correct.

Perspective drawing, or visual ray projection, is accomplished by drawing rays from the object to a point, called the station point. The rays are arrested on a plane prior to reaching the station point. This picture plane, however, can represent only one dimension of the object, and the plan view is the one usually chosen. The remaining information is obtained by additional projections and measuring devices.

Photography is the process whereby light rays from outside objects are received by the lens of the camera, which condenses them to a point. From the lens the rays of light reemerge and focus an inverted diminished image on the surface of a piece of light-sensitized film. Once exposed to light, this film is chemically developed to the point where the image on it can be comprehended as a picture of the object.

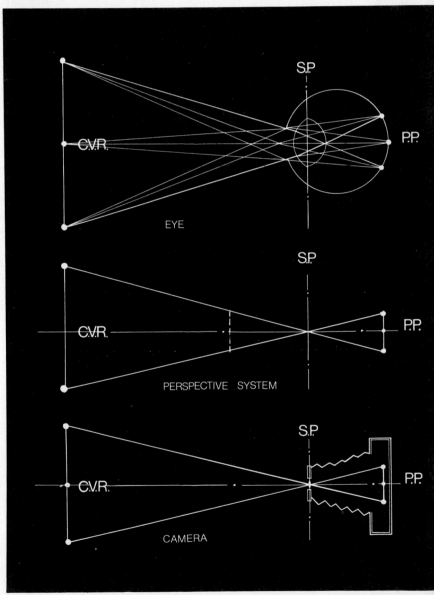

2

Any system of representation should reproduce, as nearly as possible, the eye's impression of the external world—a true representation of a three-dimensional object upon a two-dimensional surface. Neither the camera nor a mechanical system can ever do more than represent one instant of what the constantly moving eye can see. Alberti's window to the world was thus limited inasmuch as the artist could use only one eye and could not move his head. The drawing by Dürer (1) shows a device resembling an obelisk, used by artists to ensure a fixed point from which to draw. Starting from this station point, we can easily draw comparisons of the two methods of representation with that of human vision.

Station Point (SP)

That point from which the object is drawn. In human vision it is the lens of the eye. In perspective drawing it is the location of the observer, represented by a point in plan. In photography it is the location of the lens of the camera or, more specifically, the point within the lens system where the rays converge.

Picture Plane (PP)

In vision it is our picture of the object as formed on the retina. In perspective drawing it is an artificial device used to arrest the visual rays of the object before they reach the station point. It is represented in plan view by a line. In photography it is the piece of light-sensitive film within the camera.

Cone of Vision (CV)

The light-receptive cells of the retina of the eye extend in angles of 30 to 50 degrees vertically and about 100 degrees horizontally. Yet the eye gets a clear picture only within a cone of about 45 degrees. In perspective drawing it is therefore advisable to limit the cone of vision to 45 degrees, approximating what the eye sees clearly. In photography, although there is a wide choice of lenses, the kind called "normal" has a cone of vision of 45 degrees.

Central Visual Ray (CVR)

The central visual ray, or axis of the cone of vision, can be represented in any mechanical system by a straight line bisecting the angle. The central visual ray must be perpendicular to the picture plane for correct vision or representation of an object. In normal vision the system of sight is intact. In perspective drawing it is not. Here it is necessary to locate a picture plane, cone of vision, station point, and central visual ray in order to set up the perspective. It must be purposefully drawn in its correct relationship or a distorted picture will result. Although the camera is generally a fixed system, constructed so that the central visual ray will be perpendicular to the picture plane, there are many variations. Some cameras are constructed to allow changing these fixed relationships, thereby altering or controlling perspective.

3

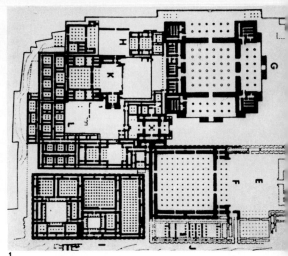

1

Photoperspectives

The delineator, whose job it is to create a perspective rendering on the basis of an orthographic plan, rarely has the opportunity to look at the plan dead on as he works from it. If he relies on the traditional methods of plotting his perspective, he will have adjusted the plan and its elevation into positions that would mechanically establish picture plane, station point, and vanishing points. But his eye is constantly seeing that plan, fixed to his working surface, in perspective. What he eventually plots, locates, and renders into a perspective drawing will actually be but one mechanical resemblance to the perspective plan his eye has seen many times and from many viewpoints.

Had the mind of that delineator the ability to freeze those impinging images into an object that he could somehow measure and scale, he would simply delineate his direct vi-

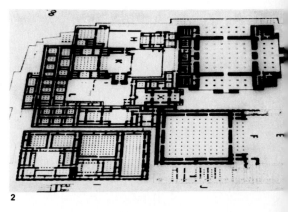

2

3

sion, unerringly, onto a new surface.

Suppose, on the other hand, that a camera had been placed at the delineator's point of view. Just as its system duplicates the physiological mechanism of the eye, so its "vision" would duplicate the delineator's vision. The plan, after all, is an object in depth when seen from an oblique angle. As previously described, the camera has the remarkable ability to create the illusion of depth of objects in space; consequently, a photograph of the plan from this viewpoint would record every subtle convergence, angularity, foreshortening of line, and diminution of scale with the same correctness as the delineator's mental vision.

In short, once the viewpoint toward the plan had been established, every existing line of it would become automatically and accurately "plotted" by aiming the camera and pushing the shutter release.

The photographed image of the plan in accurate perspective—or the "photoperspective" as it will be referred to hereafter—has abundant potential on a small piece of film. The area of importance chosen to be rendered can be selected and limited by circumscribing that area directly on the film surface. This "cropped" area can then be enlarged to the desired size of the finished drawing. The scale of the enlarged photoperspective can be determined easily by measuring some horizontal line in it and comparing its length to that same line on the original plan. Another method is to include an actual scale, like an architect's ruler, in the photo. Vanishing points can be found by tracing to convergence once parallel lines, and the horizon can be established by connecting the vanishing points with a straight line.

Capturing all this potential information on film is not a difficult chore, nor does it require the extensive technical knowledge of a professional photographer. The projects in this chapter were chosen in an effort to describe all the procedures a renderer needs to follow to make the concept of photographic perspective not only easy to use but rewarding to apply.

4

Camera Types

Subminiature Cameras

These are usually precision built and contain many features of larger cameras, such as a miniature reflex system for viewing. They are especially good for model photography work, as their small size allows them to be placed where others would not fit. The basic drawback is the small negative size, which limits enlargements in black and white. For color slides this is not a problem. Most standard films are available for subminiatures.

Fixed-lens Box Cameras

These are the most common of inexpensive cameras. The lens is ground to produce a sharp picture of anything from as close as 3 feet to infinitely far away. They are designed for the average type of snapshot and can be used for site surveys or any general picture. There is usually a separate viewing system, making critical work inaccurate. Some models do include automatic features such as exposure control.

Polaroid

These form a class all by themselves. Their unique feature is the built-in developing equipment which makes it possible to view a finished print just seconds after the shutter is snapped. These cameras are now so completely automatic that they have no adjustments at all except a simple light control. The user merely aims the camera, presses the shutter release, and proceeds to develop the picture. For general work they are quite adequate, providing a negative is not desired for future enlargements.

35mm Single-lens Reflex

With these popular cameras the user views through the lens itself, seeing the same image in the ground glass viewer that the lens transmits to the film. Focusing on a ground glass ensures accuracy for all types of work. These take only 35mm film and yield a large number of exposures per roll, making them economical for use with color. Again, the small negative limits the size of enlargements of black and white film, but for color slides this is not a problem. When a color-slide presentation is prepared, this camera is very useful for everything from site photos to critical copy work. Many accessories are available, including a variety of lenses.

Twin-lens Reflex

These widely used cameras have two separate lenses: one is coupled to a viewfinder and one takes the picture. This provides an image at all times in the ground glass and is very necessary for catching action. For other uses it is not an advantage, as there is always a chance of error (called parallax) between the two lenses. These take a larger-size film than the 35mm models and therefore are superior for black and white work. They are easy to operate and yield good results for most work. Accessories are available, such as wide-angle and Telephoto attachments.

Single-lens Reflex (2¼ Size)

These are based on the principle of the camera obscura, incorporating a mirror at a 45-degree angle to the lens, which reflects the image onto a ground glass in the top of the camera. This allows through-the-lens viewing up to the moment the picture is taken. They offer the same large film size as the twin-lens reflex, producing twelve 2¼x2¼ pictures on 120 roll film. Most models feature interchangeable lenses of all descriptions. The large, handy ground glass makes it particularly useful for certain techniques in coordinating architectural models with their sites.

View Cameras

The largest and most complex of all cameras are the view or studio cameras. They are usually limited to studio use due to their size. They can take large-size film in sheets depending on the size of the camera (4x5, 8x10, 11x14). A ground glass is mounted in a plane where the film will be inserted in holders when a picture is desired. This gives maximum quality of focusing and composing, although the image is upside down and laterally reversed. The bellows system is completely flexible, allowing the lens board, or the film plane, to be turned in any direction, thus enabling the photographer to create perspective distortion or to correct it to any degree he chooses.

Characteristics of Lenses

Most of the advanced camera types described above will accept a variety of lenses which change their angle of view. The lenses that most closely approximate human vision are constructed to receive and focus on the film a cone of light rays with an angular conical spread of about 45 degrees. These are called normal lenses. However, the term relates only to a specific camera type. For example, the normal lens for the 35mm single-lens reflex is a 50mm lens having an angle of view of 46 degrees. The normal lens for a 2¼x2¼ format reflex is a 70 to 85mm lens having an angle of view of approximately 45 degrees, and a 4x5 view camera uses a 150mm lens having the same relative angle of view.

Most wide-angle lenses cover a field of 60 to 75 degrees, although some go up to a full 90 degrees without apparent visual distortion. This type of lens lends itself to certain situations where space is limited, such as indoors or on narrow streets. It is used to capture wide panoramas or architectural models at close range. Certainly the architectural photographer must rely on it heavily.

The Telephoto lens is especially designed to photograph distant objects. The angle of view of most Telephoto lenses is from 10 to 20 degrees. It is useful when photographing a far-off site or people. However, for most applications the normal lens is sufficient and should certainly be the first lens to buy with any camera. Other lenses can be added as they are required.

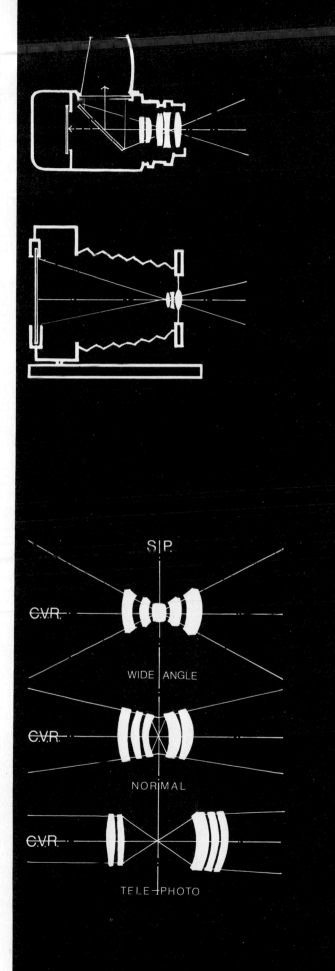

S.P.

C.V.R.

WIDE ANGLE

NORMAL

TELE-PHOTO

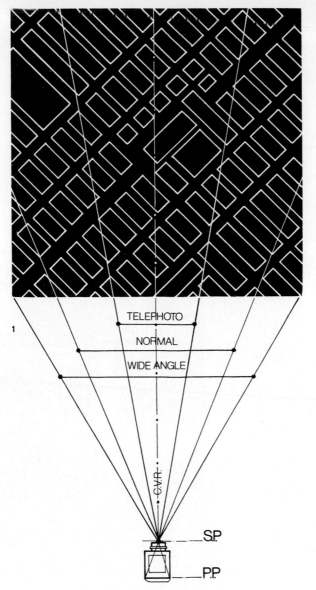

1

2

Fixed Station Point

At this point in the discussion let's put two theories to the test: one, that perspective is a function of station point, and two, that different lenses at a fixed station point do not alter the perspective appearance of a recorded view.

The diagram (1) is an actual block map of the heart of New York City. The station point for the camera was located on a rooftop several blocks away. With the camera set up on a tripod, three pictures were taken: the first through a 150mm Telephoto lens with an angle of view of 20 degrees (2); the second through a normal 85mm lens with an angle of view of 45 degrees (3); and the third with a 50mm wide-angle lens and a 60-degree angle of view (4). The three pictures were printed without enlargement, to indicate the full negative image. Then a section corresponding to the Telephoto frame was selected from each of the other two and enlarged to the Telephoto frame. The outline on these pictures indicates the area that was enlarged. It further illustrates the extent of enlargement of that area due to the angle of vision of each lens. The resultant three photographs (5,6,7) are identical. As long as the station point remains fixed, the three lenses will produce identical perspective images.

The second experiment was made by using one lens and changing the station point relative to the object. Three views were taken (8), each successively closer, and all three were enlarged until the object appeared the same size (9,10,11).

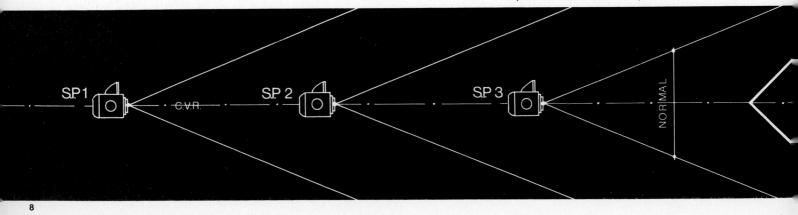

8

3

4

5

6

7

The view from station point 1 is flat with very little convergence and is similar in appearance to what we might expect from a Telephoto lens. The flatness is due entirely to the distant station point. The view from station point 2 is normal with a reasonable degree of convergence and looks like most images of structures we see every day all around us. The view from station point 3 is somewhat distorted in appearance, similar to what we are told to expect from a wide-angle lens. The extreme convergence is due only to the close station point. In short, perspective is the direct result of a single element: station point.

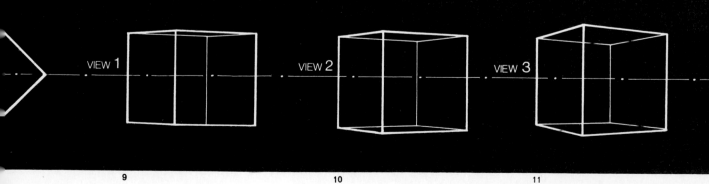

VIEW 1   VIEW 2   VIEW 3

9   10   11

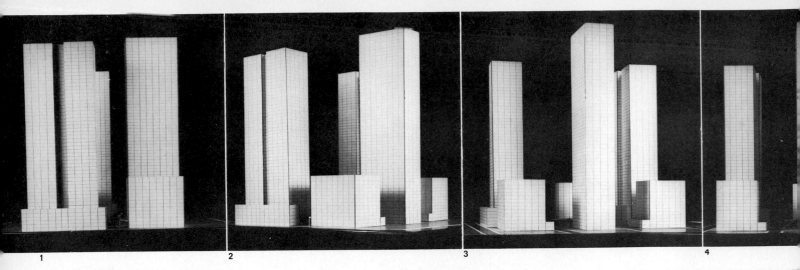

1 2 3 4

Changing Station Point

Architecture is fixed, immobile, and unchanging in form. To an observer, however, the appearance of a structure does change, because the observer is capable of motion. Therefore, the observer is the one who must be considered in any attempt to show a structure from different vantage points.

The changing relationships experienced by a person walking around a structure can be duplicated very easily. An architectural model was used to represent a group of buildings in a city block, and a camera to record the views of the observer. The model used was a box model of simple cardboard construction. On the surface was drawn a grid representing a curtain-wall window system.

Two photoflood lamps were used to illuminate the surface and a black backdrop was put behind the model for contrast. The camera was set on a tripod and elevated to a height that would approximate the eye level of a person walking around the building. In order to ensure a constant station point, the camera was fixed in position and the scale model was pivoted about its center point. This produced the same effect as if the camera had been on a circular track and circumscribed a complete arc around the structure. The results can be seen in the series of pictures above. Commencing from a flat, head-on view (1), the model was rotated,

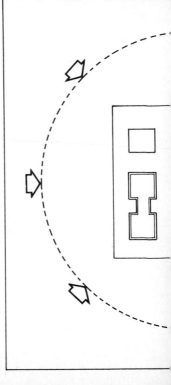

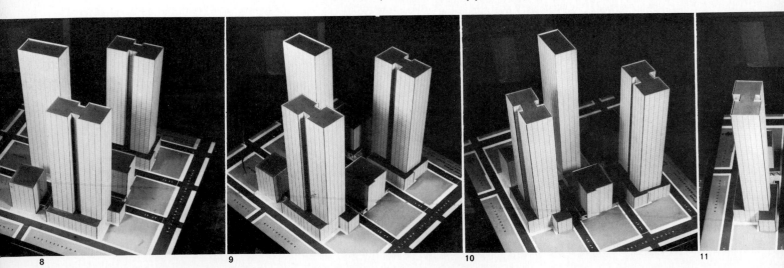

8 9 10 11

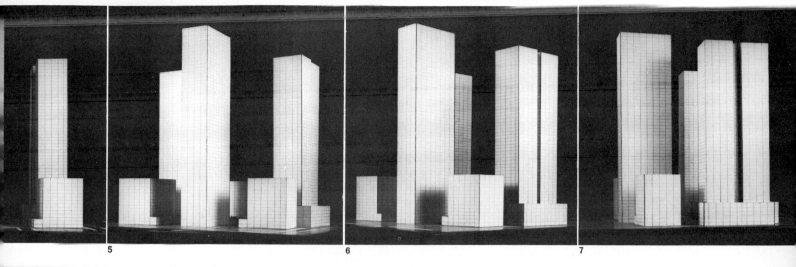

5   6   7

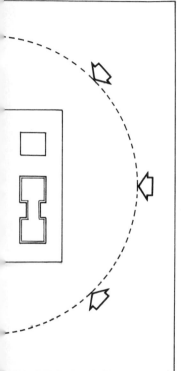

producing several oblique views (2,3). At one-quarter of the way around the model, another flat, head-on view (4) was recorded. Moving further around provided two more oblique views (5,6). Finally, at one-half the distance around, a view was recorded that was directly opposite to the first (7).

Studying the interrelationships made possible by the use of the camera should be an exciting change to the delineator. Previously he would have laboriously set up a perspective, only to find that a few more feet to the right or left of his chosen station point would have produced a more desirable result. To the architect wishing to study his project this exercise is invaluable.

The same demonstration was done for a high viewpoint. The camera was placed on an elevated tripod at a fixed distance from the model. In the same manner as before, the model was rotated through 180 degrees and a series of photos was taken (8–14). From this high station point the camera was tilted away from perpendicular, producing a third vanishing point. The result of this exploration will show you what to expect from the camera. You might even begin to consider exciting angles of perspective you would have hesitated to try before now. Do not feel restricted to a ground-level viewpoint. The three-point results you capture on film are as easy to work with as the conventional perspective.

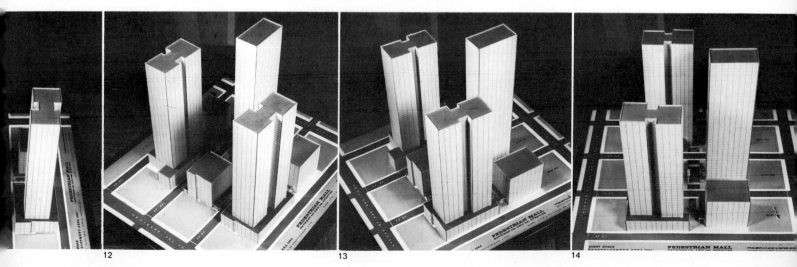

12   13   14

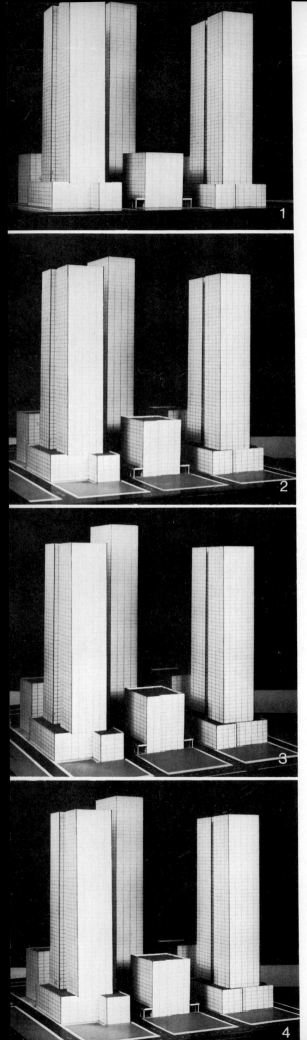

1

Eye Level

In the previous example the station point was kept constant and the camera positioned before the model was rotated. Remember, station point as a symbol occurs only in a plan view, whereas eye level occurs only in elevation. The two are inseparable. Station point represents your distance from the structure as measured orthographically in plan view, and eye level means your height above the station point, which can be measured only in elevation.

From a selected station point you might want to study the effect of a changing eye level. With a camera and a model of a proposed project this is a relatively easy matter.

The camera was placed on a tripod which had an elevator head capable of moving up or down with a crank. It also had the elevator shaft calibrated into equal increments to facilitate measuring the eye level. The results are shown here in four consecutive views (1), each an equal distance from the previous one in height. The camera itself had to be kept parallel to the vertical plane to avoid introducing a third vanishing point (2).

As mentioned earlier, the human eye is a closed system. All things look "natural" to the eye because that is our standard of judgment for "seeing." When we look up, things diminish upward, and when we look down, things converge downward (3). Yet this never bothers us because we are always within our frame of reference. However, when a photograph duplicates this process (of perspective convergence), we find it noticeably disturbing because it is outside our frame of reference. Therefore, a picture of what our own eyes see can be disturbing unless we view it from the correct distance and at the proper angle. This means from the same relative position that the camera was when it took the picture. Then the picture will appear normal again to us because it is much like the way we would see it ourselves.

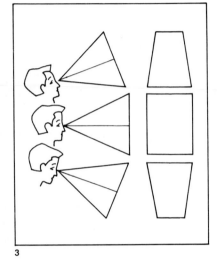

2

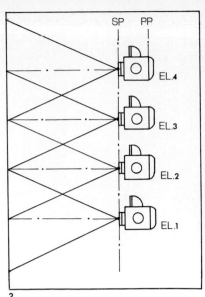

3

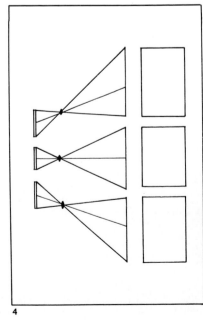

4

5

7

6

Any time the camera (4), and hence the film plane in the camera, is tilted out of a plane parallel to the object, a distorted looking picture will result. The vertical lines will appear to converge to a third vanishing point. This is a natural manifestation of perspective. The upper edge of the building, being farther away from the lens, will be accordingly smaller. There are ways, however, to avoid this. If the camera is held horizontally, distortion will not result, but the picture will not show enough height and will include too much fore- ground. The camera in the same position but with the lens raised will give a perfect photograph of the whole structure.

The camera most commonly used to control this situation is the view camera, having a lens which can be raised or lowered and tipped or swung. However, the two views shown here (5,6) (7,8) were taken with a 35mm camera with a special perspective control lens which can be raised or lowered. Normally such features are available only on larger cameras.

8

1

2

3

4

Camera Movement

People view most action in real life in terms of four basic sequences: the distant view (1), medium view (2), close-up (3), and extreme close-up (4).

A rendering is limited to one view from one location at a time. However, with the camera you can explore many possibilities within minutes. Viewpoint is no longer restricted to what is convenient or mechanically easy to construct.

When exploring a model, site, or building for possible viewpoints, consider these basic elements of the simple sequence: the distant view, the medium view, and the close-up. To these can be added the extreme distant view and the extreme close-up. In a sequential form these basics produce pictorial continuity, which may have little significance for the single rendering, but becomes the criteria for slide and film presentations.

The view which establishes the scene is the distant view. This can sometimes be very far away, locating an object in its surroundings. The medium view would be a "normal" view, usually encompassing the entire object or building within a well-balanced framework or composition. While the distant view is quite elastic, the medium view has little range and becomes sharply limited to the full-view or full-figure shot. It is also known as a transition view between the distant and close view.

The close view is more revealing of detail. It necessarily has focused on only a portion of the entire project, emphasizing entourage. This close view can also be stretched to an extreme close-up, or environmental view, where great attention to detail is necessary. The object has lost its frame of location and becomes immediate environment. In the sequence shown, movement was kept in a relatively straight line, as one would walk toward a building, up the street, crossing the street, and terminating with the main focus at the entrance. This is the basic formula of the simple sequence.

5

7

Perspective Systems

There are three systems of architectural perspective drawing. One is known as one-point perspective (5), where the object is parallel to the picture plane and those sides of the object that are at right angles to the picture plane recede to one vanishing point, while everything else remains parallel.

6

Another is known as two-point perspective (6). This system assumes a vertical picture plane upon which all vertical lines of the object appear vertical and parallel while all horizontal lines converge to vanishing points on a horizon at the same height as the eye level. Three-point perspective (7) assumes a picture plane inclined from vertical. Systems of horizontal lines still converge to vanishing points on the horizon, but now only the vertical line which is intersected by the camera axis remains vertical, while all other vertical lines converge to a vanishing point along this line. There are three vanishing points for systems of lines parallel to the three-coordinal axis.

1

Shades and Shadows

Linear perspective is a conventional way of representing three-dimensional objects on a flat plane. In actuality buildings and other objects never exist merely as linear outlines. We always see them as surfaces. Some are transparent, some opaque, but all are differentiated by varying tones. A photograph will record all forms by their relative values on a scale of tones ranging from black to white. These tones will appear different as the intensity and direction of light changes. Textures which appear smooth in flat lighting might become quite bold under strong crosslighting.

To study some of these changes, a series of pictures was taken of the same building at three different times of the day and from three different locations (2,6,10). The linear outlines of these three different views describe how the shapes would appear without definition of tone. The series of photographs demonstrates morning light (3,7,11), midday sun (4,8,12), and late afternoon sun (5,9,13).

Certain academic knowledge of plotting shadows is certainly necessary for the proper execution of a rendering. However, the selection of values in the distribution of light and shade is equally important. Often this is purely a matter of judgment. Studying photographs of actual lighting conditions on different shapes, surfaces, and materials will certainly add to that vocabulary. One of the easiest ways to accomplish this is to study photographs of buildings in periodicals. Or you might want to try your own camera on a particular case. The pictures shown here were taken with a Hasselblad fitted with a 185mm Telephoto lens at a distance of approximately 300 feet on Tri-x 120 roll film. Exposures were 1/250 second at f/16.

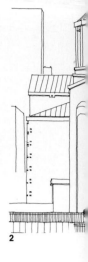

2

6

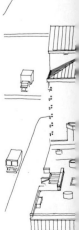

10

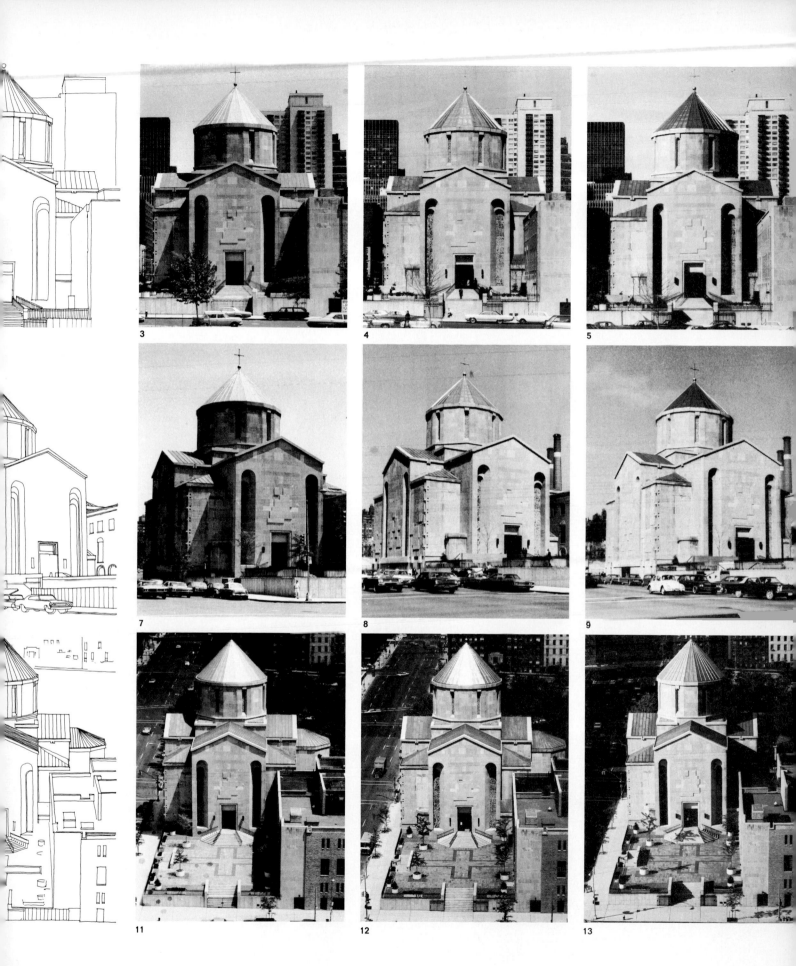

1

2

Aerial Surveys

Once you have decided to accept an assignment for a project requiring a site-coordinated aerial layout, you should check available sources for photographs. You will need to know where they can be obtained, how much they will cost, and how quickly you can get them.

There are three main sources for obtaining aerial photos, one being the commercial aerial photographer, the second a commercial photographer who will take an aerial assignment, and finally, yourself. The services of a commercial aerial photographer will vary from city to city. This man's business is usually to keep an accurate record of the city's development in his area. In most cases he will have taken strictly orthographic views for map-making purposes. His camera is mounted inside the airplane and his equipment is specifically designed for aerial photography. In smaller communities this is the extent of his services, and he would have no other photographic records you could use. He would fly a special assignment for you, but he would most likely wait until he had several assignments to cover in one flight. However, if you have the

3

4

5

time, this is the best possible source, since you would get sharp, accurate pictures that could be used for many purposes. In larger cities, each aerial photographer has a more diverse file. If you buy a picture from his file, you are buying only the print, as he retains the negative and charges you for use only. This is the most economical way to obtain high-quality pictures for your own use.

If you cannot find the exact picture you want from any photographer's file, you can hire a photographer willing to take an aerial assignment. He will use more conventional cameras and film, but his work may not be any less expensive than the aerial photographer. He will expect his usual fee plus the expenses of hiring the plane and pilot. Unless he thoroughly understands what you expect, do not be surprised if his pictures are not taken from the exact angle you had in mind.

If there is no alternative except to take the pictures yourself, some preparation would be in order. You can practice for your aerial venture on the ground. Have someone drive you around town while you take stills from the moving car. Use the car method to get used to switching from camera to camera and to practice loading and unloading film. You will find that once you are airborne, the most simple task seems to take three times as long as it did in the studio.

You might want black and white pictures for enlarging and color pictures for slide projection. In this case a 35mm camera would be wisest for the color and a 2¼ format would be best for the black and white. Do not take a bellows camera, since the wind will tear the bellows right out. Taking two cameras is much easier than changing film in midflight.

For aerial surveys the helicopter has many advantages over the small cabin plane. In either case the door will have to be removed for good clear pictures.

Before departing, make sure you have plenty of film handy and filters on your camera for haze. Even on the clearest day, the haze, not visible from low altitudes, becomes a serious problem. It tends to degrade the photographic quality of the image by reducing its contrast. The effect of the haze differs with the angle of the sun, so if you are taking a series of pictures circumscribing a site, some will show different contrast than others.

While on the ground, familiarize your pilot with your assignment. Use a road map to draw your intended flight pattern around the site. Try to find landmarks such as the two water storage tanks shown in the sequence here. These will guide you and the pilot in finding the site.

Start shooting before you reach the site. This not only provides you with some lead-up material, it also will get you used to the aerial shooting experience. The first noticeable distraction will be the noise of the craft, causing you to wonder if your camera is working. For the first time you will not be able to hear the shutter click as usual. Don't bother to focus, set the camera at infinity, and don't worry about depth of field.

The shutter speeds required are necessarily high, generally 1/250 to 1/500 second will stop the effect of movement. Don't brace yourself against the aircraft, but isolate the camera from any movement.

Finally, remember that no matter what attitude the aircraft is in, the horizon must appear level in the picture or it will look unnatural. In a helicopter this is sometimes a problem, since the craft is not always absolutely level in relation to your site.

The whole ordeal may take only 30 minutes to an hour for most flights within close range of the airport or heliport, and this would not prove too costly. What you will get, usually, is something of value, since you were in control of most of the decision making.

Careful development and storage of this film will be added precaution that your aerial photographic expedition will continue to prove worthwhile in the future.

6

7

Computer-Plotted Perspectives

The sequence of computer-plotted perspectives for the University of California Medical School dramatically demonstrates the flexibility of the computer. It is also capable of plotting the most complex shapes, including land contours. The accuracy of the computer is astounding, but its main advantage is that it can create these images in a fraction of the time it would take to draw them.

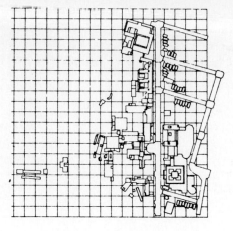

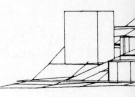

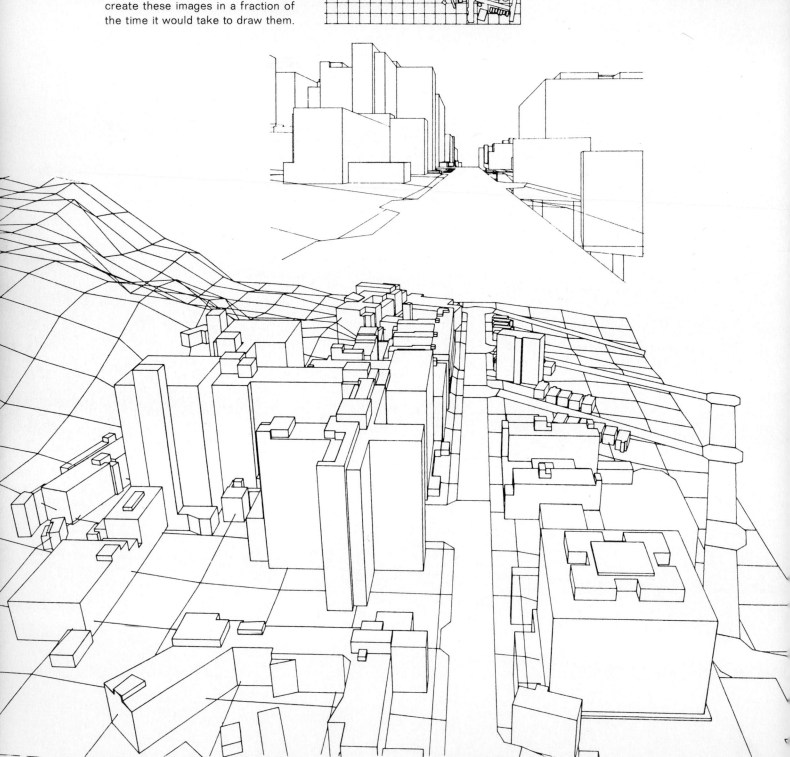

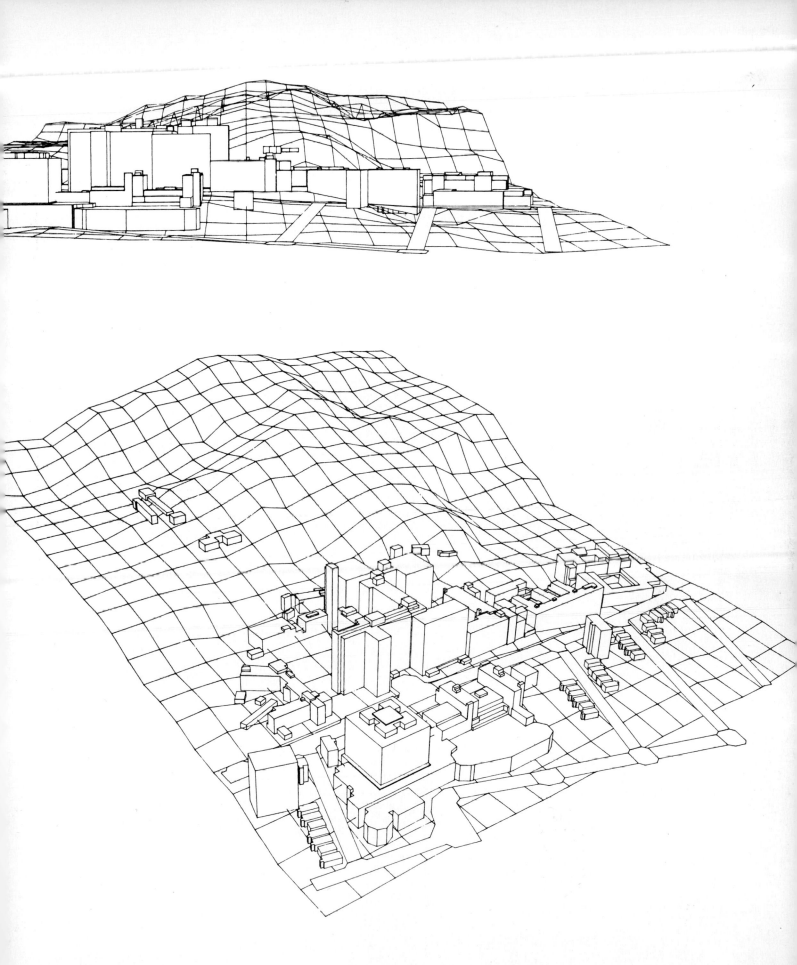

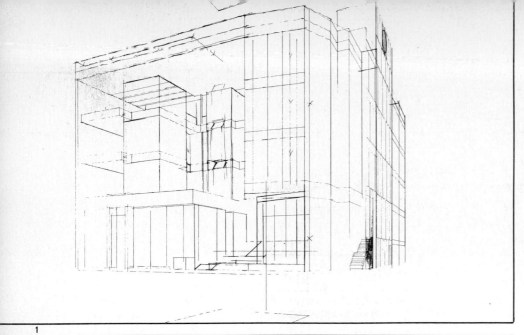

1

2

3

Computer-Plotted Layouts

Once a layout is produced by the computer (1), it can be developed into a rendering just as can be done with any other method. Details can be added using traditional measuring techniques (2). At this point, it can be traced onto a board or used with an overlay to produce the final drawing (3).

**Layout by the Illustromat Computer
Drawings by: Scheffer Studio**

LAYOUTS: FROM PLANS AND MODELS Chapter 2

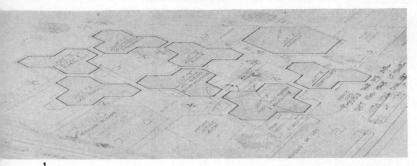

1

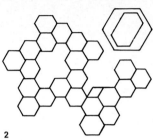

2

West High School

The orthographic plan (2) of this high school reveals an arrangement of geometric shapes that appears difficult to plot using conventional methods. The photoperspective, on the other hand, makes it look relatively easy. The shapes of all the units, in perspective, were plotted simultaneously by the camera (1).

Many photographs had been taken, to determine the best possible relationship of forms and the most pleasing composition. The picture chosen for enlargement had two sides of the six-sided figure parallel to the picture plane (3). This left two other pairs of sides for which vanishing points had to be plotted. Vanishing point right was located on the drafting table. Vanishing point left, however, was so remote that diminution toward it was practically nonexistent. As a result, all lines receding to it were traced as parallels. Working with this plan led to a reevaluation of some of the techniques normally employed in creating a perspective drawing. Were vanishing points really necessary?

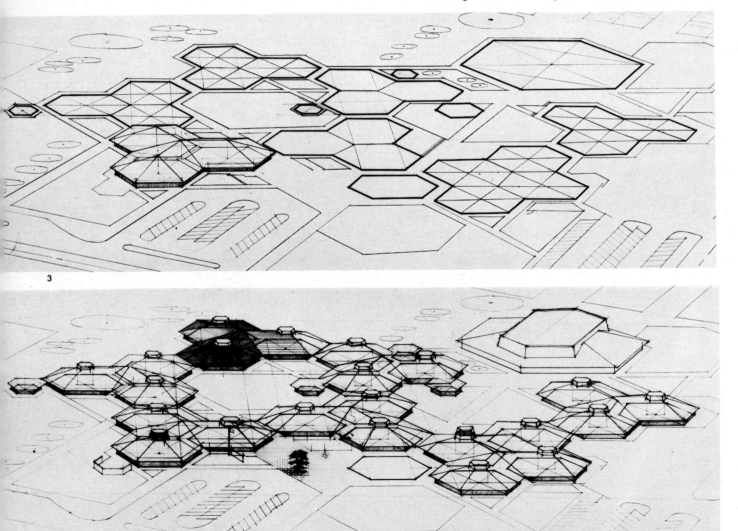

3

4

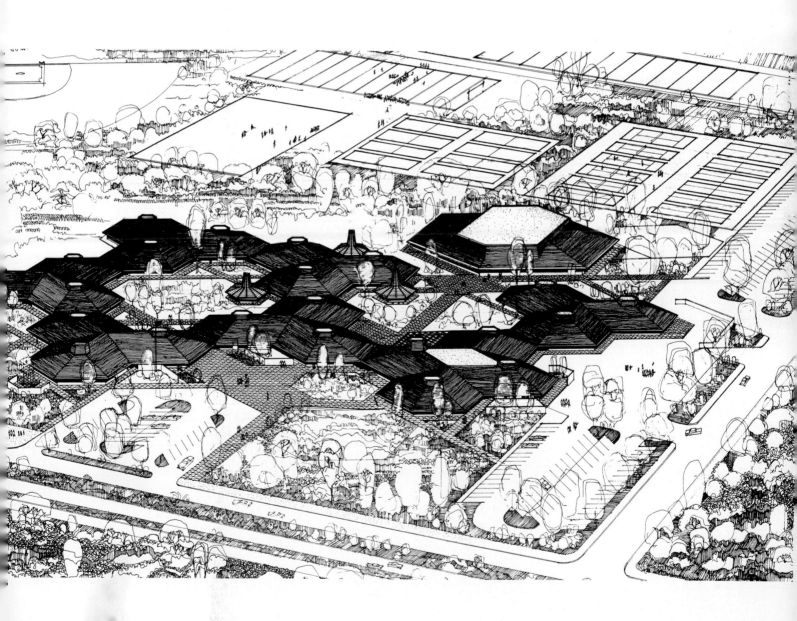

1.

A — 1/8 SCALE — B — 1/4 SCALE — C — D

A — 1/8 SCALE — B — C — 1/4 SCALE — D

2.

A — B — C — D

A — B — C — D

3.

The Custom Grid

The basic tool of the photoperspective is the custom grid. It is not a perspective grid in the common sense of the word, since it does not "diminish" as other grids do. Diminishing is "built in" to the photograph of the plan in perspective, and the grid will also be in perspective. Rather than a grid on which measurements can be taken, it is simply a guide for converging lines in one, two, or any number of directions.

Vertical heights can be scaled on any portion of the plan by simply selecting a line in a position parallel to the picture plane and measuring it against the same line on the actual plan. A ratio will thereby be established between the actual line *AB* on the photoperspective and the one on the drawing *AB*. Any height can then be found easily at that point. If any known height at the foremost portion of the grid is traced back, following the converging grid lines, it will be the correct height anywhere in the perspective. If this same line were traced back to the point of origin, it would enclose a geometric shape.

To establish the grid, simply take any two originally parallel lines from the photoperspective (1), preferably the nearest and the most distant, and extend them to each edge of the drawing on the left. You now have a trapezoidal shape (*ABCD*) with one side shorter than the other. Select a scale such as $1/8'' = 1'0''$, and place the scale vertically to the horizon. Mark equal division between *A* and *B*. On the right side select a scale slightly larger, such as $1/4'' = 1'0''$, and place the scale in such a manner that you arrive at the same number of divisions between *C* and *D* as on the left side. Now connect point for point each corresponding number (2,3). This grid shows the perspective convergence to the left vanishing point. The same procedure will establish a converging grid for the right vanishing point. You now have a custom grid—tailored to your photoperspective—and from that grid you can determine the convergence of each and every line of your drawing.

4

5

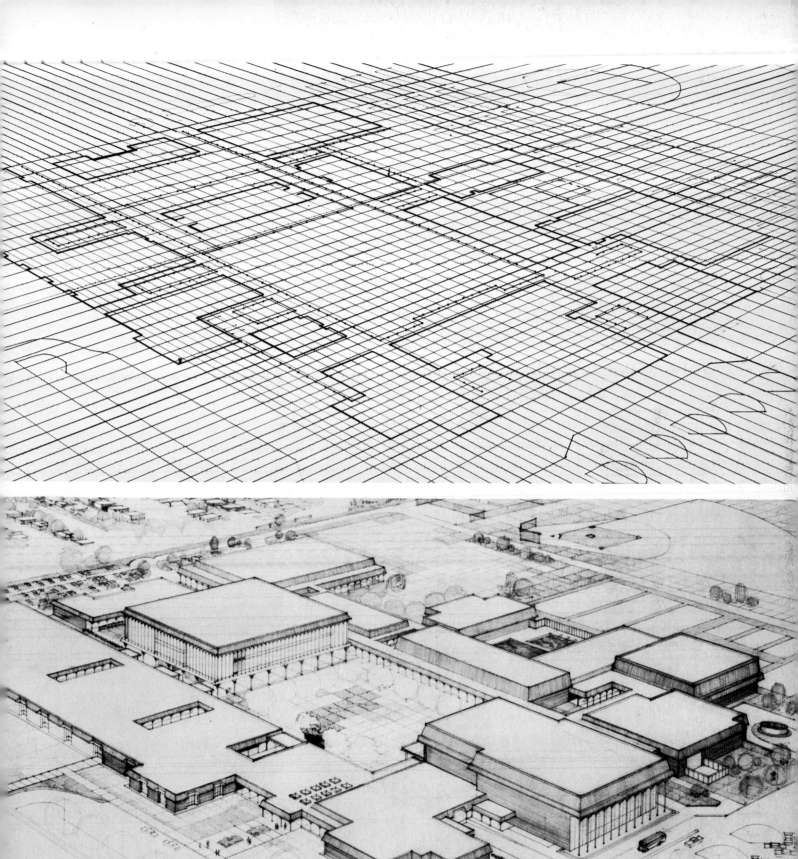

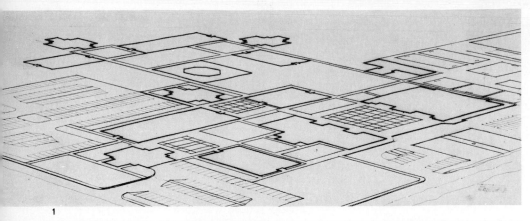

1

Vanden High School

A rectilinear plan naturally lends itself to establishing certain guidelines for the execution of a layout (1). The plan itself, as seen in the photoperspective, is already a perspective grid. Therefore, any line added to that plan can be placed there, using the existing lines as a guide (2). From this simple beginning an entire rendering can be constructed without the use of vanishing points (3,4).

Care must be exercised in photographing the plan to ensure that background forms are not obscured by those in the foreground. This can be overcome by taking several pictures using an elevated tripod.

After a vertical scale has been established on the photoperspective, all vertical elements can be projected up from their point in plan. Then the roof configuration of each structure can be roughly sketched in. Next an accurate layout is made over this rough outline and the location of trees added before commencing with the final ink rendering (5).

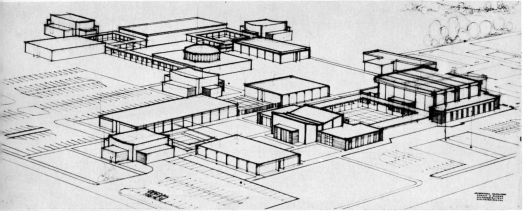

2

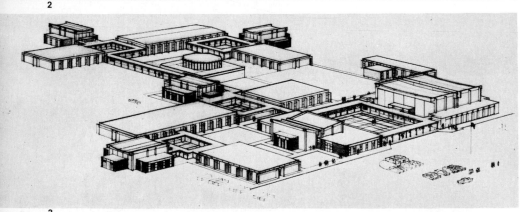

3

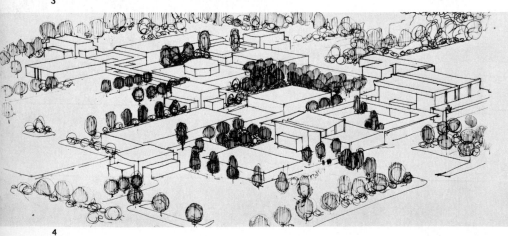

4

5

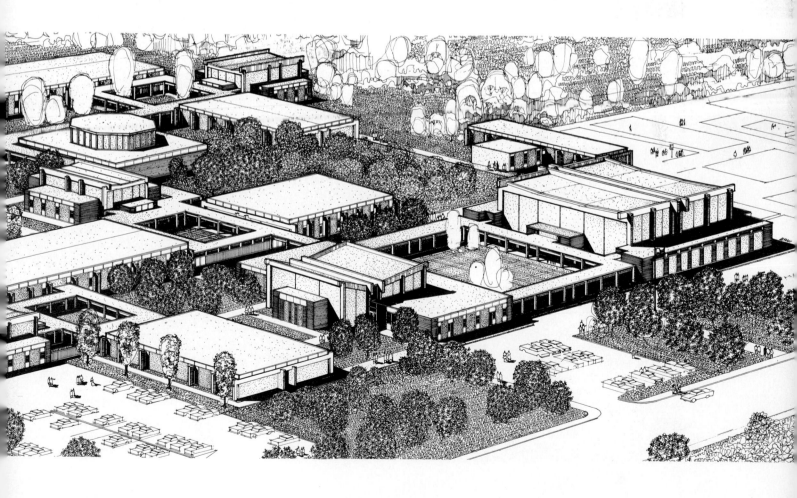

1

Camelback Inn

2

This organic arrangement of pentagonally shaped units would have given the most experienced layout draftsman a difficult time. No aspect of the plan could be called a frontal or a lateral view (2). The problem was to determine an aesthetic balance of the masses without destroying the plasticity created by the linking of the units. This difficult problem was also solved simply by the photoperspective (1).

Several pictures of the plan were taken from different angles and varying heights. The compositionally "right" (3) view was almost immediately apparent. The negative selected was placed in a mount and the image was enlarged to the desired size, using an ordinary slide projector. The plan was projected onto a piece of paper taped to the studio wall, and the outlines of the plan were traced in pencil onto the paper. This tracing became the basis for the perspective drawing.

Each pentagonal unit was turned slightly from its neighbor so that vanishing points were totally useless. Therefore, each unit was treated as a separate drawing and linked together to create the total picture (6).

4

5

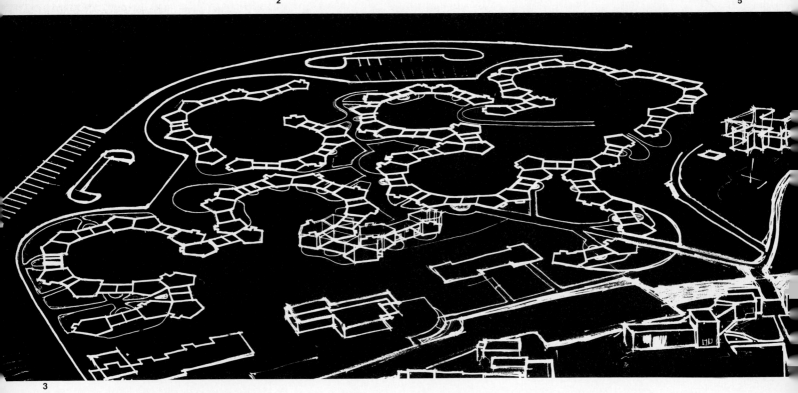

3

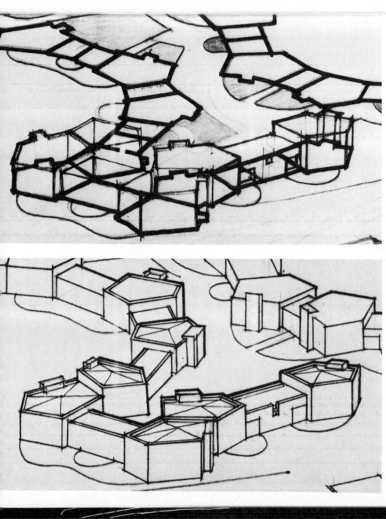

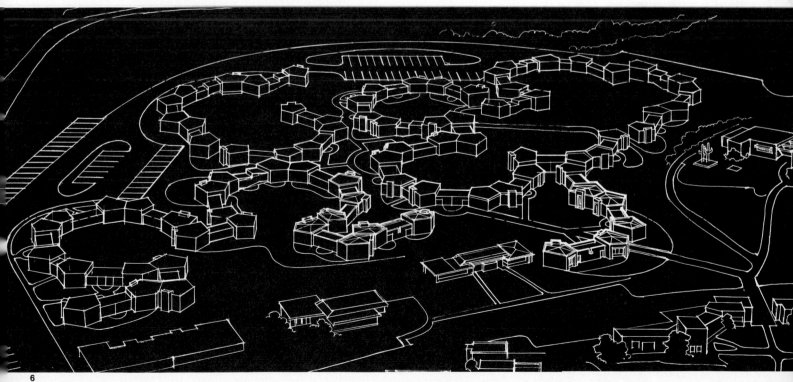

6

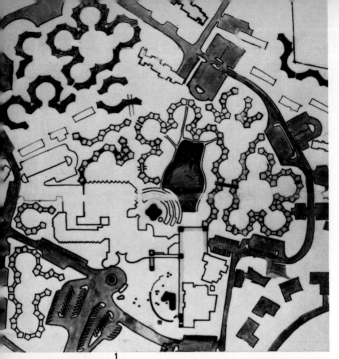

1

Camelback Inn

It is not rare that one has the opportunity to do a drawing of an addition to a project that has already been built. The unusual aspect of this project is that the original rendering was completed by the author 10 years earlier. The original layouts are on pages 38 and 39, and the buildings now occupy only a small area in the upper left-hand portion of the new version (1). Once the original designs were built, the entire resort site was photographed from the air (2). This aerial photo provided the guidelines for the new rendering. Using the process described on page 104, an acetate sketch was put over the ground glass in the camera and the photoperspective was taken (3). This was traced onto paper and a more detailed layout was done in pencil (4). The photo technique for this project was an indispensable tool for accurately locating all the odd forms in their true relationship. The final layout of these new buildings was done using techniques identical to those described in the original project on page 38 (5). The final color drawing was executed on a sand-colored board, using magic markers for the background, ink and white tempera for the highlights (6). The color drawing is on pages 30–31.

Drawings by: Ernest Burden

5

2

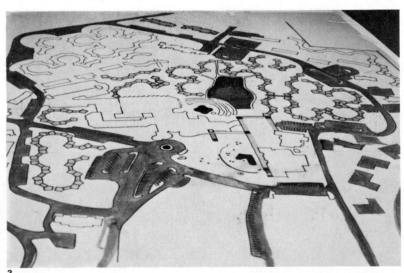

3

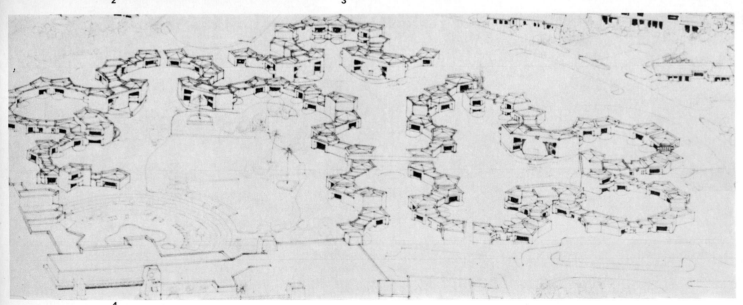

4

6

40

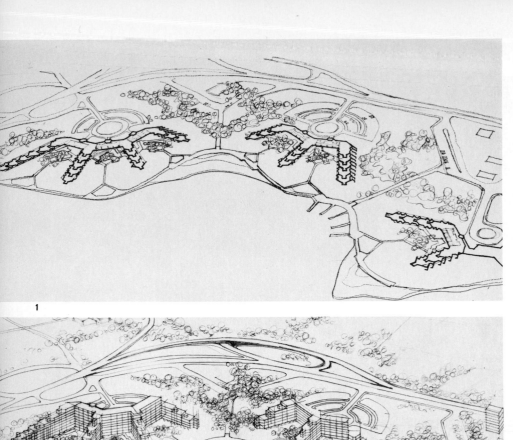

1

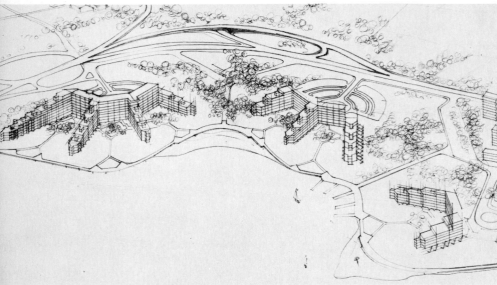

2

Some structures are complex not only in plan, but equally in elevation. With the photoperspective (1) of the plan the verticals can be projected to whatever height necessary (2).

First each exposed side of the structure is built up floor by floor much like an isometric drawing (4). Diminution and convergence are negligible, due to the distant vanishing points. Next, the balconies are projected from each of these floor lines and windows added where necessary (3, 5). If handled in this fashion, the whole (7) will not be any more difficult than the sum of its parts.

6

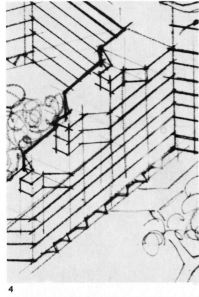

4

3

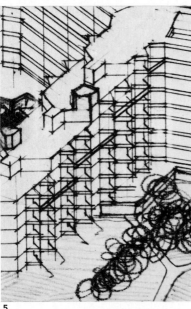

5

7

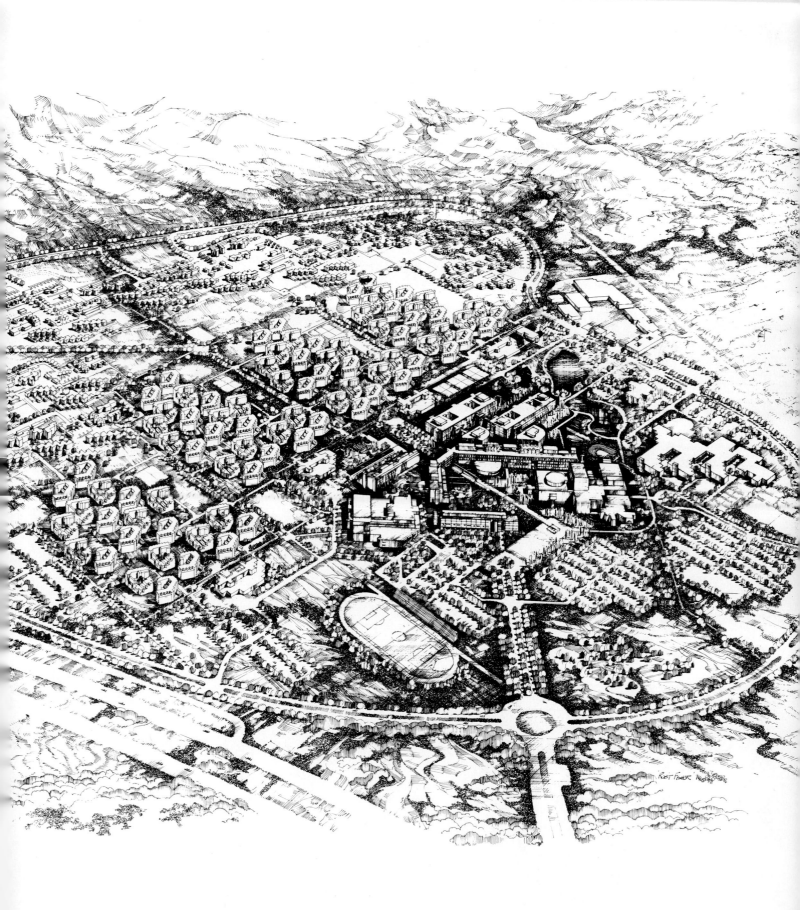

Types of Models

1

5

Stage Set—Type 1

The simplest of models can be constructed from the architectural drawings, preliminaries, or sketches. These drawings are simply pasted on cardboard and set up like props. This model is built only where the camera will see it, which can usually be determined beforehand. The cardboard model represents only one plane of the structure, which is perfectly adequate for most projects.

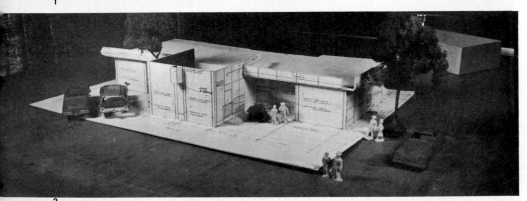

2

Stage Set—Type 2

Similar to the type 1 stage set in that the elevations are pasted on cardboard, it differs in that additional elements can be added to create depth. Roof overhangs can be added as well as projections of any kind. Scale figures and scale automobiles can also assist in getting a more realistic preview of what the drawing will be like.

3

Structural Cardboard

Usually employed when it is desirable to see into a structure, this model is much more complex to build. Contours are easy to build out of cardboard, provided the scale is correct. Models of this type are even less difficult to build out of Styrofoam core board.

4

Interior Model

This is truly a stage set in every sense of the word. It can be built with or without ceilings, and usually three interior walls are advisable. If there are columns or obstructions in the room, it is a good idea to put them into the model. They can be quite a distraction if they are not placed properly.

9

Contour Model

The model for land shapes can be made easily by utilizing cardboard for the contours as opposed to the expensive machine-milled Styrofoam contours associated with presentation models. Visually, this type of model is best suited for slide presentation use, as it is too elaborate for rendering purposes.

6

Box Model

A simple stage set model is carried to completion, by constructing all sides and enclosing it. This adds a solidity to the model and is more reliable for larger buildings where true vertical is desired. The main advantage is that any number of views can be taken from any angle, since it is a complete model. However, it should be constructed without an investment of time, since it will probably be disposed of.

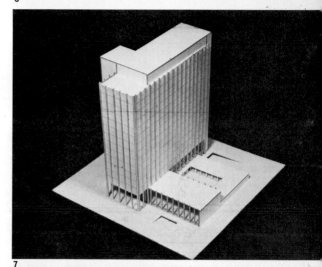

7

Mass Model

This is similar to the box model in that it is complete in three dimensions. When shapes are too complex to build from cardboard, a solid form is easier to use. Again, the elevations are pasted over this form. The mass model, because of its solidity, tends to be more accurate than the cardboard, and corners and uprights tend to be true.

8

Presentation Model

Used primarily for slide and film presentations, it must be well built but is still not in the class of models built by professional model makers.

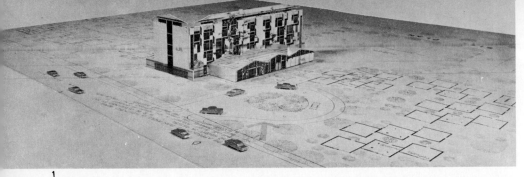

1

2

Rosewood Estates

Some plans may contain a combination of forms, some of which may be easy to project up from the photo-perspective, and others which are relatively simple in plan but complex in elevation.

To overcome this, you can combine a semi–stage set model with the plan, as was done for this project (1). The elevations were pasted onto cardboard and put up as props, leaving the rest of the plan on a flat plane.

Since the elevation represents projections on a flat plane, the cardboard stage set represents only that one plane. The balconies which extend from that plane had to be projected out. The actual distance was determined by proportioning (2).

The small housing units flanking the larger structure were simply projected up from the plan, using methods previously described (3, 4).

3

4

Two Firehouses

1

2

3

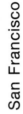

4

5

6

The more complete a model is, the greater the advantage in using it to prepare a layout. If a model has been built for another purpose, you can still use it for your perspective.

In the two examples here the architects had already built study models, both of structural cardboard so that you could see into them.

In the San Francisco firehouse the interior of the structure was clearly visible from a low viewpoint. This is a little more elaborate than what is usually required to do a perspective. Some information was taken from the plans and elevations, but mostly from the model (1,2,3).

In the Berkeley firehouse project the model was not as carefully constructed, yet all the essential elements were there. It is quite an easy matter to straighten up the various planes on the pencil layout and to locate the vanishing points at that time. Any revisions to the drawing can be easily and quickly made at this point using the information available from the model photo. The major benefit to the cardboard model is that it provides more information than the single-plane, stage set model (4,5,6).

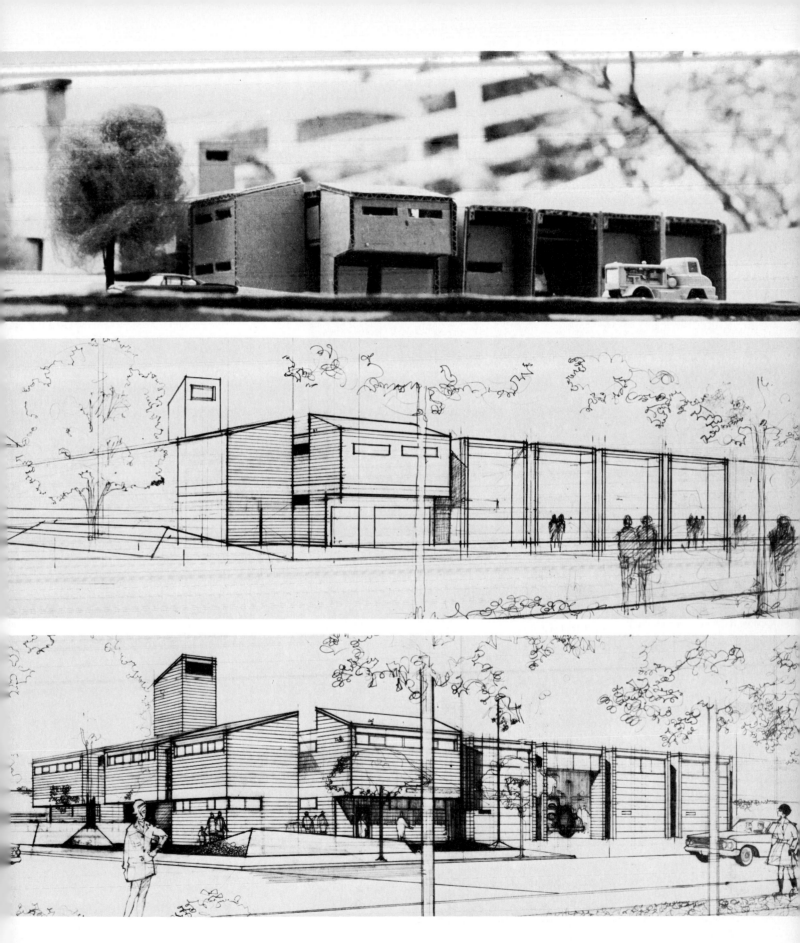

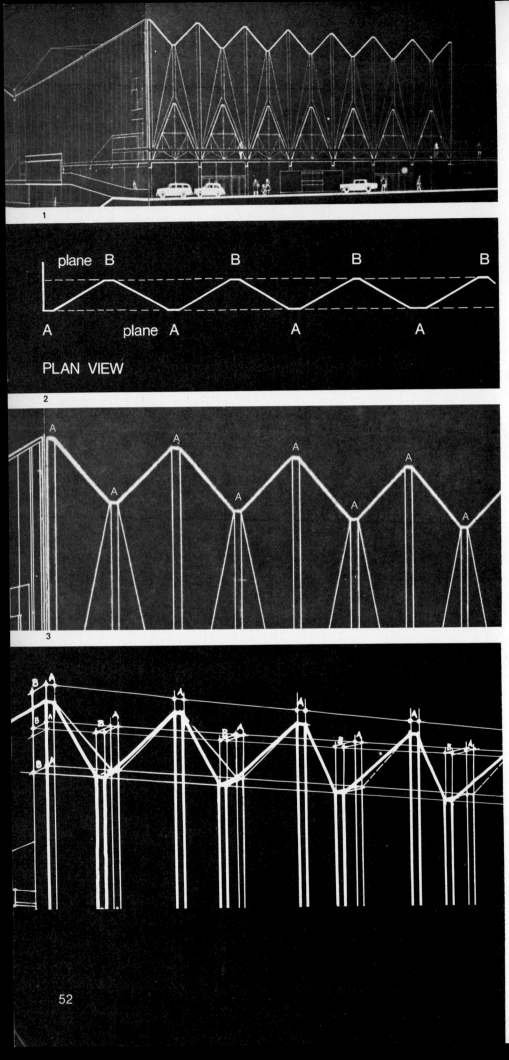

plane B   B   B   B

A   plane A   A   A

PLAN VIEW

Civic Auditorium

When drawn in plan and elevation view, most structures can be described by certain fixed planes. These planes are easy to represent by utilizing simple cardboard forms. More complicated structures, however, require certain adjustments in order to make full use of the photographic technique (1).

You could spend a little additional time building the model to conform more closely to an irregular shape. You might find it easier, however, to consider everything as being projected onto a flat plane, such as the elevations, and build a simple model representing those planes. After the picture is enlarged, you can project objects in front of, or in back of, these preselected planes.

After the plans and elevations for the coliseum shown here were studied, it was decided that the simple model would supply information for the layout. The front façade of the building was, in plan view, much like the pleats of an accordian or camera bellows. In elevation, of course, the pleats were all flattened onto the same plane. This meant that certain lines that were not in that plane would have to be located by other means.

The plane of the front façade is denoted by the letter A. The inside plane is denoted by the letter B. To find plane B in the photograph, you simply measure its distance back in plan view (2). Call this distance X. By projecting plane B in plan view to the outside wall, you can determine exactly where it falls in elevation. Mark this on the enlarged photograph of the model (3,4).

The peaks of A remain where they are in the photograph since they are in the plane of the model. The valleys must be projected back to plane B as shown in (3). With this established, the rest of the layout will fall right into place (5,6).

52

4

5

7

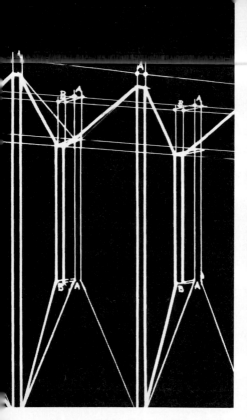
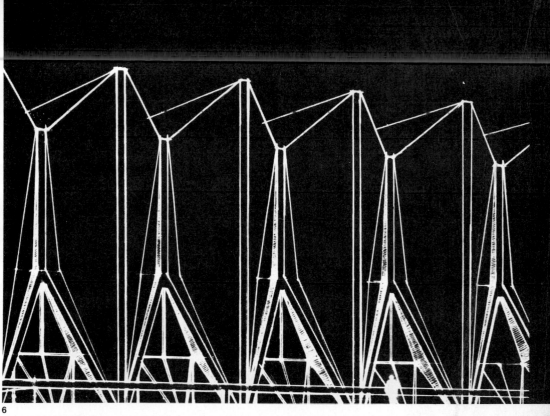

6

1

IBM Cafeteria

Whenever the ceiling of an interior space is an important feature in the drawing, it should be included in the model. The scale of the model should be at least ½ inch to the foot.

The ceiling pattern was created by drawing one typical bay to scale and photocopying it 18 times to make up the entire ceiling pattern (5).

Since the ceiling was more than 12 inches from the floor, lighting was not a problem. The camera had to be placed outside the model to obtain the proper eye level. Toy figures were placed at random inside the model to give a sense of scale to the interior space (1). After the photograph was enlarged to the desired size, two overlays were made on acetate. The first one completed the arrangement of figures and furniture (2), and the second completed the ceiling pattern (3). One of the unique advantages of this particular model was using it to create two renderings: the first of the cafeteria and a second of the lobby area immediately adjacent to it. Since the structural ceiling was the same for both areas, the only thing needed for the lobby view was two walls. The ceiling was reused (6,7).

5

3

4

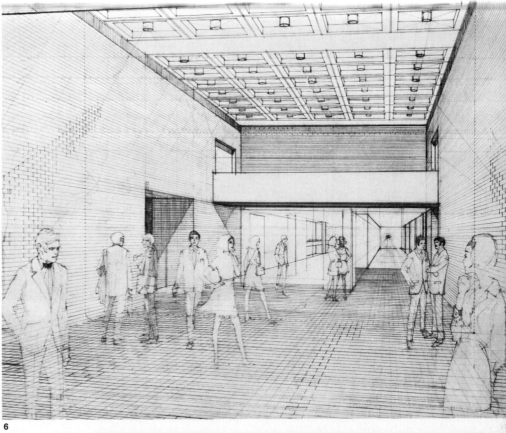

6

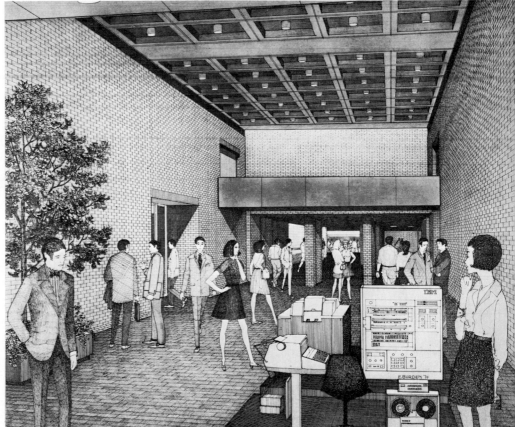

7

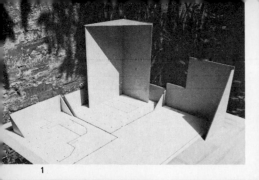

1
2

3

American National Bank

There is little need to build the areas of the model which the camera will not see. Once you have decided on the possible viewpoints, you should build the model to satisfy only those conditions (1,2).

For this project the elevations were drawn on tracing paper with a heavy ink line to indicate floor heights and window divisions. This paper was pasted onto cardboard, cut out, and assembled into a simple stage set model (3). Props were used behind the façade to keep each side upright, and the corners were reinforced with a triangular cardboard piece to ensure right angles.

The model was then taken outdoors for photographing, as photofloods were not available at the time. This provided very even illumination on the sunny side of the building but tended to obscure the detail on the shady side. However, the detail was sufficiently clear upon enlargement to use the negative.

When one of the vanishing points is off the board, you can construct a grid to give you the proper convergence. On the right-hand side of the drawing, construct a vertical line and mark off equal increments on the $\frac{1}{4}$-inch scale between points A and B. Next, take this same number of increments on the $\frac{3}{8}$-inch scale and move the scale, held vertically, back and forth until the same number falls between A and B. Then connect each corresponding number on the two scales. This will give you the true perspective convergence to a distant vanishing point on the right (4).

4   5

1

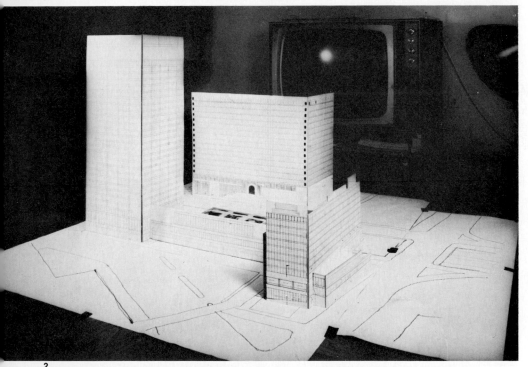

2

Gateway

The model is a valuable tool for the perspective artist, but certain precautions should be taken when photographing a group of stage set models. These are not as accurate as more elaborate models and are sometimes difficult to align properly. When arranging a group of buildings on the plot plan, it is hard to judge by eye how accurately they are placed. Even a slight error can be bothersome when enlarged.

To compensate for this, a custom grid is used to ensure that everything in the drawing will converge in the same plane. It is much easier to correct the alignment on the drawing board than it is to worry about perfect placement of the elements on the plot plan.

In this case, photographs of two separate models were combined to produce the final layout. The one used to obtain information for the background was the architect's early study model. The stage set model represented the latest design of the structures and was constructed in the studio. The two negatives were then enlarged by projecting them onto the same piece of paper, to the same size and to the same scale. Then the grid was drawn over the entire drawing to make certain that the background buildings and the project structures were in alignment. After this was accomplished, the drawing was carried to completion.

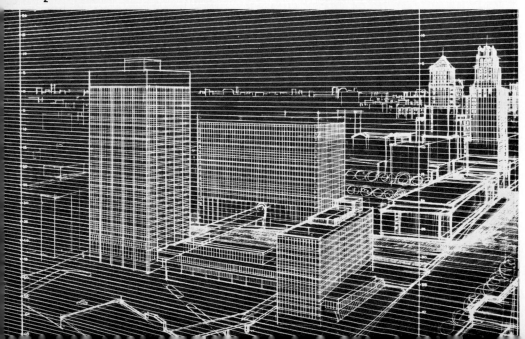

3

4

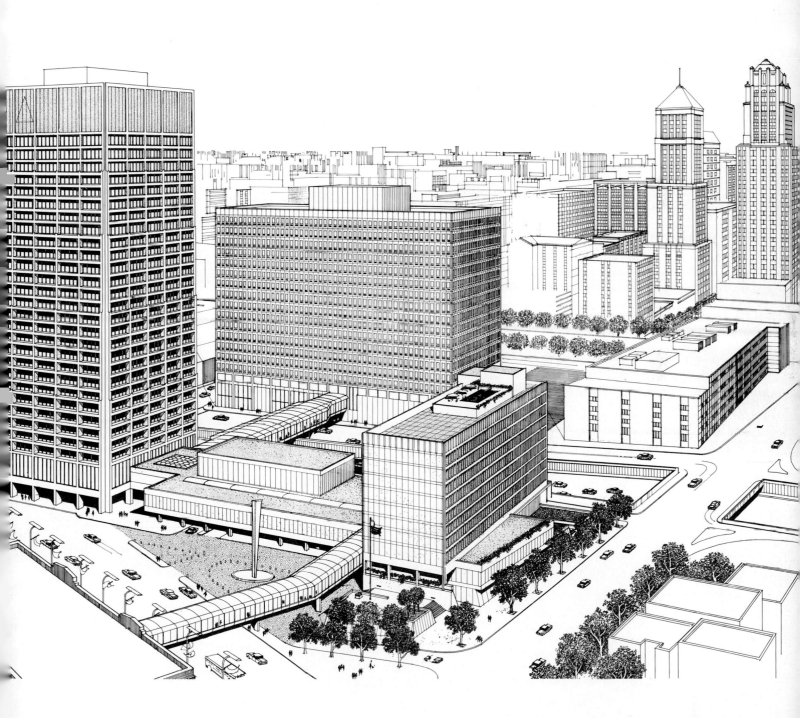

1

Gateway

Cardboard study models often serve more purposes than they were originally intended for. If such a model exists, you can use it to advantage even if it does not contain all the detail you would like. Lacking from the model shown here (1) were lines marking the horizontal division of the walls of the long low hotel unit in the foreground into precast units. The floor levels were indicated in the rough model. To find the panel divisions horizontally was relatively simple. A vertical line was drawn at the corner of the building and, using a convenient scale, the exact number of horizontal divisions were marked off along the vertical line AB beginning at the point labeled zero (which could have been located anywhere convenient on AB). Next a line labeled C was located at the opposite end of the structure representing the end of the divisions.

There were 54 divisions in the length of the elevation. This was broken down into 9 major divisions and 6 minor divisions within each 9. These were laid off vertically at the near edge of the building represented by the line AB. Then each division was projected toward the vanishing point on the right side. Since this was off the board, a custom grid served the same purpose. Then a diagonal was drawn from B to C. The intersections of this diagonal with the 54 divisions going toward the vanishing point gave the perspective diminishing dimension to each panel unit. All that was required then was to drop each intersection perpendicularly down to the surface to be divided.

2

Bunker Hill Towers

Naturally, the more complete the model, the easier it is to create perspective renderings from it. With such a complete model as the one shown here, many different approaches are possible. Several views were taken in order to study the relationship of the lower pyramidal structures to the towers in the background. In photographing such a model, you may introduce a third vanishing point by tilting the camera if you do not have perspective controls on it. However, this can be easily corrected on the drawing board by choosing a plane at the horizon line and using the dimensions at that line, make all the verticals straight. For additional guidance you can establish a custom grid over the elevations.

1

2

3

4

5

6

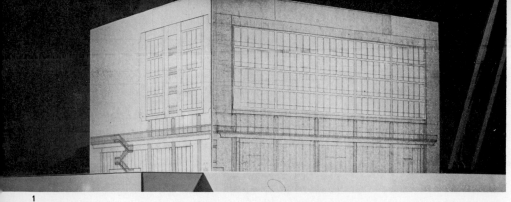

1

2

Model to Site

A rendering is like an anticipated photograph of the completed building, and if the completed project is photographed from the proper angle, it should compare well with your rendering.

In the examples here, three projects were visited after the structures were built. The results indicate the comparison that can be made.

In the first sequence, the model was a simple stage set made from two pieces of cardboard set at right angles to each other. The elevations were pasted onto the cardboard. The plane of the cardboard was the plane of the outside surface of the precast concrete window panels. Therefore, the windows, being recessed from this surface, had to be projected back a small amount.

The plaza ultimately extended to the right of the building rather than to the left as in the rendering. Other than that there is very little difference between the rendering and the completed building.

The third example is one where the actual site was photographed prior to executing the rendering. There was no attempt to coordinate any particular view of the existing features with the new structure. Therefore, the picture of the completed structure differs from the rendering in the positioning of the foreground tree. This was initially taken from a different position, yet added to the drawing to give depth and scale to the drawing. The following chapter describes the advantages that accrue when you visit the site with the express purpose of coordinating the site with the new project.

3

4

1

Foley Square

When the buildings that are adjacent to your project are askew, it is difficult to plot their location (1). Besides, the details on those buildings would have to be recorded from free-hand sketches or guesswork. With the aid of the camera, even an inexpensive one, you can achieve both detail and accuracy (2).

Once you have the site pictures, you will be far ahead of the situation in terms of constructing a layout. The site will dictate to a large degree what is possible and what is not (3). While the site should not intrude on the building itself, it should be an integral part of the rendering. The model can then be photographed quite easily using the same technique as that described on pages 96 and 97 (4). Once you make the site picture, whether it is a single shot, a multiple shot, a panorama, or a mosaic, you simply enlarge the model photograph to fit the site. You can do the same procedure in reverse if you have an existing model photograph as your source; that is, fit the site to the model.

The more the site and model are coordinated with each other in scale, angle, and detail, the more useful the total drawing will be to the client (5). The final color drawing can be found on pages 36–37.

Drawings by: Ernest Burden

2

3

4

5

Commercial High School

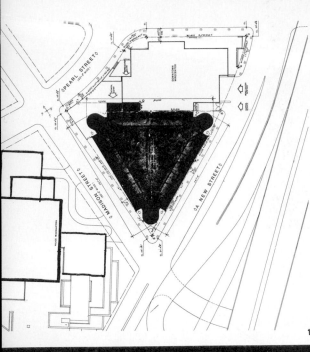

A rectangular building on an irregularly shaped lot can be a challenge when one is trying to determine a perspective viewpoint. But consider the unlimited possibilities of a triangular building on a triangular lot surrounded by existing, nonrelated structures (1). In addition, a neighboring 60-story office tower and the off-ramps of the Brooklyn Bridge add to the complexity. If you want to explain the triangular shape, you might be tempted to show it from above, but that viewpoint will lead you into the situation where the background becomes a more important consideration than the building.

The site survey for this project is unprecedented in its approach and thoroughness. Three different views of the site were taken from varying levels. For each different viewpoint, the model was photographed using techniques described on pages 96–97. Prints were made to scale and pasted over the photo of the site (2). Even though the model was a rough cardboard study, the final look of the rendering was very visible—so visible, in fact, that all aerial schemes were abandoned in favor of a ground-level viewpoint which focused on only the building (3). The city background gave it realistic scale but became quite incidental (4).

1   2   3

VIEW FROM CHATHAM GR. · HIGH ·

VIEW FROM MUNIC. BLDG. · HIGH ·

VIEW FROM PACE TOWER · HIGH ·

VIEW FROM CHATHAM GR. · MED ·

VIEW FROM MUNIC. BLDG. · MED ·

VIEW FROM PACE TOWER · MED ·

VIEW FROM PACE TOWER · LOW ·

VIEW FROM CHATHAM GR. · LOW ·

VIEW FROM MUNIC. BLDG. · LOW ·

VIEW FROM BACHE · LOW ·

COMMERCIAL HIGH SCHOOL · STUDIES FOR VIEW APPROVAL
ARCHITECTURAL DELINEATIONS BY ERNEST BURDEN · SEPT. 30 '71

4

5th and Mission Garage

One of the great perplexities in architectural photography is the control of objects unrelated to the principal subject. Only a small number of these distractions can be removed by the architectural photographer. A delineator, on the other hand, can select what he chooses to include in his rendering. If the appearance of overhead wires is detrimental to the photographer's picture, he must either choose a different viewpoint or remove them from the negative. In a rendering, however, it is an easier process: you simply chose those elements of the site you want to use in the drawing and eliminate the rest. In the rendering shown here the only items that were eliminated were the overhead trolley wires. Whatever you do include, however, should have some purpose to it. This would include items that either determine scale, help provide depth, identify the setting, or lend atmosphere to the drawing. Without one or another of these elements, site coordination would not be necessary.

1

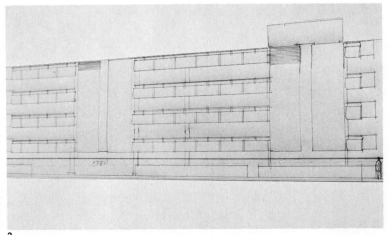

2

3

4

5

Berkeley High School Cafeteria

The decision to do a site-coordinated rendering can come from some seemingly unimportant request, such as to include a recognizable representation of an existing bas-relief sculpture from a nearby existing building. In order to photograph the sculpture, it was necessary to go to the site and take pictures. Several photos were taken of the sculpture on the building during school hours to avoid interference from the students. However, the decision to stay and take additional photographs as the students changed classes provided the real basis for this combination of photograph and drawing. It provided a picture that produced this totally candid scene. The students were unaware that they were to be included in a rendering. In addition you can always find students around who will be more than happy to provide you with any pose you might want.

1

3

2

Initially the purpose of the photographs was to provide a picture of the relief sculpture; however, upon seeing the results of the excursion in print, it was decided to render the building into the photograph rather than paste pictures on the rendering. And this is exactly what was done. The existing building on the left, the students on the plaza, and the actual plaza itself are photographs. The building was rendered to the proper size separately (3), cut out around its outlines, and set into the photograph. Trees were added as well as foreground planters to soften the harshness of the plaza. Unfortunately the trees were not yet planted when the picture (4) of the actual constructed cafeteria building was taken. In the rendering, one large, unattractive building in the background was eliminated, as it appeared to interfere with the importance of the primary purpose—to illustrate the new cafeteria building and its relationship to an existing structure, a plaza and a bas-relief sculpture.

4

1

3

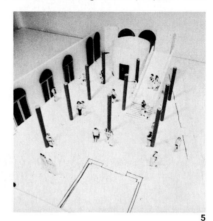

2

5

4

Cooper Union

This layout had to be coordinated with the site because the site was the existing interior of a building under renovation. Pictures were taken of the empty space (1), wherever possible. Rough sketches were drawn showing the new studios in use. Photographs of students from previous art classes were available from the student photo file (3, 4). These showed the students working and discussing their projects and were a valuable resource to complete the sketches.

Some of the areas, such as the new lobby (5, 6), were not accessible for photographs. Layouts for these spaces were done by building ½-inch scale models including the ceiling. Columns were important to include since any view, if not chosen carefully, could be obstructed by too many columns. The columns were made from round, stubby pencil erasers. They were held in place in the styrofoam floor and ceiling by a pin inserted into the soft eraser center.

Sketches of figures drawn on cardboard were cut out and placed around the model to give it scale and to add a realistic look to the otherwise barren model pictures. This addition would also make the choice of view more meaningful (7).

Two views looked promising and were enlarged for layout purposes. However, upon a closer look, one layout was discarded because the staircase was not prominent enough.

In the drawing of the painting studio, the existing photograph (8) was quite helpful in setting up the background for the drawing (12). First, a rough sketch was used to locate the various elements of the room (11). Again, pictures of students at work were used in the layout. The natural quality and unassuming poses were perfect for this use (9, 10). The finished drawings in this series are shown on pages 214 and 215.

8

6

9

10

11

12

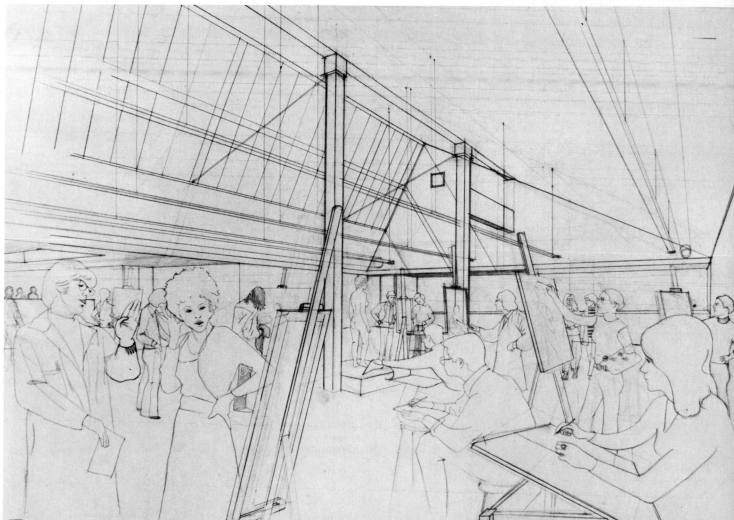

7

1

3

4

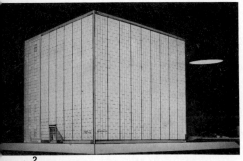

2

▲ VIEW 1
▲ VIEW 2

2

Pacific Tel and Tel

Both additions to existing buildings and future extensions to new buildings call for some form of coordination with an existing situation. Occasionally you might even encounter both in the same project. In addition, you might desire more than one view of this addition to an existing facility and its future extensions.

First the camera is used to record the existing building or at least features of the building that can be useful in setting up the perspective. Next a model is built which indicates the relationship of the new structure to the existing one. The site photo becomes reference for the elements of scale such as figures, cars, and trees, and the model is reference for

the detailed information on the building itself.

Each negative is enlarged to the same scale by using the existing building, which is shown in both the site photo and the model photo, as a measure. These are then traced onto the same piece of paper.

When the initial phase of each view is completed, the drawing is sent out to a photographer and a photographic print of it is made, leaving enough blank white paper to allow space for the rendering of the new addition. This planned future addition is then drawn as a continuation of the photograph, and if this is done in ink, the technique will look identical to that of the initial phase.

1

3

4

5

5

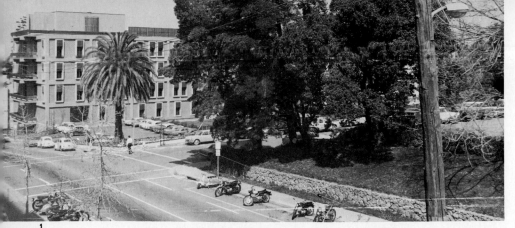

1

2

Etcheverry Hall

The requirements for this project, an addition to an existing building, left very little room for maneuvering. The existing building had to be shown in some way, however small. The open courtyard between the two new classroom wings had to be clearly expressed. Finally the eye level should not be higher than the roof of the proposed addition. These requirements fixed a station point and eye level that would have been very easy to satisfy, but for one primary requirement—that it relate to the existing structure.

After the approximate station point was located on the site plan, it was evident that an oblique view across the street would provide just the right view, if the height above the ground could be managed. Fortunately there was another classroom building from which pictures could be taken. Permission was obtained to take the pictures during class break, and a series was taken looking from several different windows toward the site. In the studio the pictures were studied for their relative height and position. Similarly the photos of the model, taken with the aid of an acetate diagram on the ground glass to determine the view, were studied to see how they corresponded to the site photos. Certain target points provided assistance: the horizon line was obtained from the site photo, and the location of the corner of the building determined the inside corner of the existing sidewalk.

From the set of model photos one was found to meet all the requirements of the client. The two negatives were then placed in a projector, enlarged to the size of the finished drawing, and roughly sketched out. After this procedure a more detailed layout was executed in pencil. Many different approaches could have been taken to render this building; however, no other viewpoint would have satisfied the specific requirements imposed. Fortunately, with the aid of the camera these restrictions were not difficult to work with.

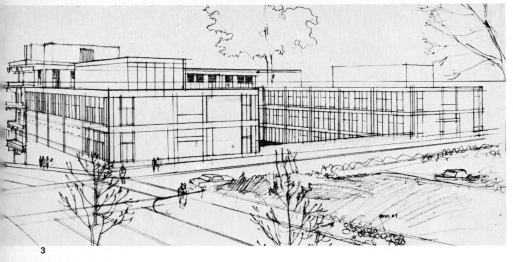

3

4

5

During the design stage of a project several design variations on the same structural scheme may come up for comparison. You could make a separate rendering for each scheme if the building were not too elaborate or the project warranted the extra time and expense. An alternative to this approach can be found in a site-coordinated layout.

The first step is to select a viewpoint favorable to each scheme. Next, select some site photos and project them up to the desired size. The site is drawn up to the point where the actual building will be placed. In this case, the site was quite long, requiring much background work. Then the drawing was sent out and two photographic prints were made from this site drawing. Each layout was then transferred to its respective photograph and the rendering completed as usual.

Kaiser Hospital

5

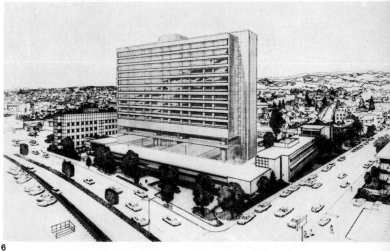

6

Milvia Center

One of the advantages of being able to study site and model together without difficulty or wasted time is that you can quickly see any flaws that might show up in the finished product. This is particularly true when you want to experiment with unusual viewpoints such as these rooftop views. First a number of photos were taken of the site from the most available rooftop, across the street from the proposed building. Of the several studies made, two things were apparent. First, the composition would be unnecessarily dull from that angle. The problem of equal emphasis on the sides of the building was apparent, and it was therefore discarded as a rather poor choice of view. The second view was not much of an improvement since it faced the wrong direction and showed only the intersection of streets and a few adjacent buildings. The rooftop idea was quickly dropped when a study made from the street level was constructed. In each case certain aspects of the site were traced on acetate, placed on the ground glass of the camera, and moved into position to photograph the model from the same station point as the site. The street view not only provided a more interesting composition of the building itself, but gave the opportunity to show some identifying surroundings.

7

1

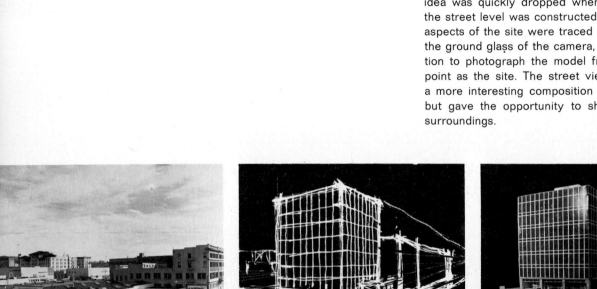

2

3

4

5

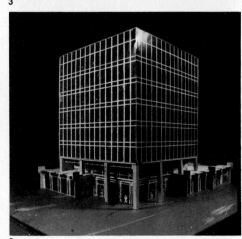

6

10

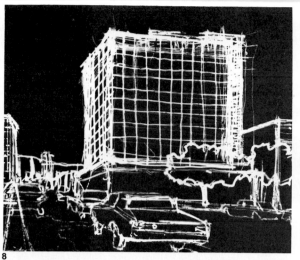

8

9

Charles River Station

This lock-control station was designed to resemble the structure of a bridge, yet the building was placed adjacent to an existing bridge. The concern was to keep the bridge from appearing as part of the building.

The rough cardboard model was photographed on a table. It was apparent that this building could have been on dry land. What was lacking was the reflection. This problem was solved by placing a large mirror underneath the model.

The bridge in the background was drawn in ink line, then scratched evenly with an Exacto blade to break the line into finer dots and dashes.

Westchester One

Sometimes the site and the model do not fit together like hand and glove, and you will find that some patchwork is necessary. Trees can be rearranged in the foreground, figures can be added, and distances can be shortened or lengthened within reason. This activity is no different from rearranging the elements in a sketch fashion, except that by using photos, you can maintain an accurate scale (1). All these diverse elements will be unified in the layout stage where each element can now be related to one drawing (2).

2

Lincoln Plaza

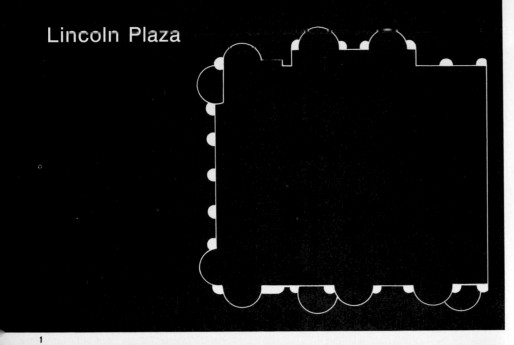

1

2

3

Circular forms are always a problem for the perspective artist. Imagine then a series of exposed round structural columns, semiround bay windows intersected by circular balconies, repeated throughout 30 floors. Each circular element for each floor level would be a different ellipse from its immediate neighbor. This would be true for the entire height of the building. It was a wise decision, then, to build a model accurately enough to determine the true positions and relationships of these circular forms.

When the columns were measured in plan, it was discovered that standard half-round wood moldings would be perfect in size. These can be easily purchased at any lumber yard. They were glued onto the elevations, which had been previously taped down to a table. An architectural feature, a concrete band at all floor levels, was provided by using black tape, which is available in many widths. This was wrapped over each of the wooden half-rounds at each floor level. The balconies and bay windows were a little more of a problem due to their large size. However, cardboard tubes provided the answer here. The tubes were cut in half and placed on the elevations. The floor heights, windows, and sills were all drawn flat on a piece of paper then cut out and glued around the tube. Now everything was represented just as it would be in the final structure, except with cardboard and tape. Yet each curve was there, clearly visible.

It would have been a shame to have put all this work into the model without consideration of the environment of the proposed structure. A time was chosen late in the day to photograph the site so that the sun would be very low, which would provide good detail on the existing buildings.

To photograph the model from the same station point required the use of a 4x5 view camera with a rising front. There would be no way to include the top of the building without tilting the camera, thereby distorting somewhat all those hard-earned ellipses.

4

5

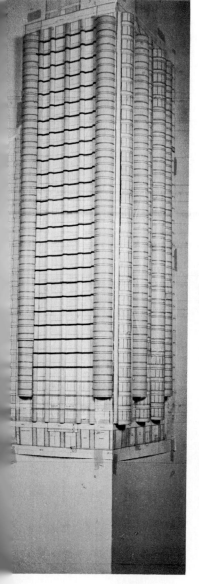

6

1

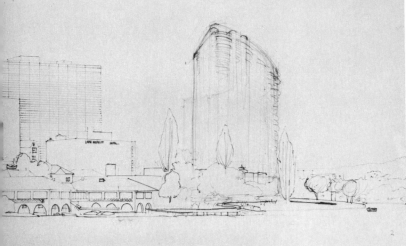

2

Lake Merrit Apartments

If you already have a model built for study purposes, you might be tempted to see how your new project will fit into the environment. So without any elaborate preparations you might go to the site and take a few site photos and, by approximating the same conditions in the office, take a few shots of your model. By enlarging the site negative to the desired size of your rendering and enlarging a photo of the model to the same size, you can see at a glance whether or not this is the best viewpoint (1,2).

In the case here, two things were apparent. First, the background buildings were strong design elements and dominated the drawing. If these buildings were left out, there would be no need for site considerations at all, since only the new building would show. Second, the apartment was to be located on a circular corner lot at the edge of a lake, and this relationship was not at all apparent in the view studied. The model and the site were then rephotographed from an aerial angle to show their proper relationships (3,4,5).

3

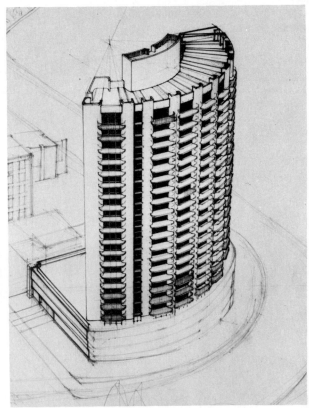

4   5

90

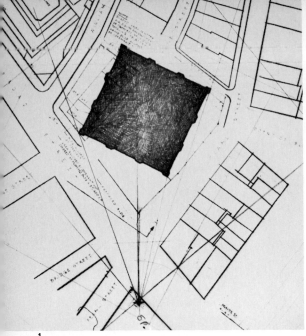

1

2

3

Project Downtown

In order to create a truly convincing coordinated layout, you may find certain conditions stretched to the limit. Thus far the sites have been relatively convenient and easy to photograph. From studying the site plan, it was obvious that there was only one spot from which to see the structure pictured here and relate it to the space around it. In addition, the closeness of the station point resulted in a 60-degree wide-angle view of the model alone.

However, since the building completely separated the site left from right, an extreme wide-angle perspective of approximately 100 degrees was attempted. The site on the left was taken on one negative and the site on the right was taken on a second negative. Keeping the lens at the pivot point helps maintain perspective control. Since not all the streets and buildings were at right angles, any minor variations not only would pass unnoticed but would be meaningless.

The limited cone of vision of 60 degrees applies to the building vertically as well. This means that from the desired station point the camera could "see" only to the fourteenth or fifteenth floor. However, with the information obtained from the model photo the actual vanishing points were found. The top of the building was plotted by an extension of the floor-to-floor heights then these were projected to the vanishing point.

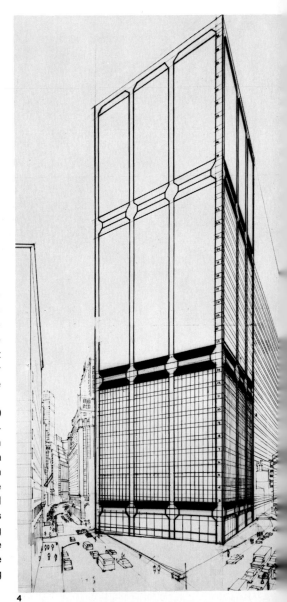

4

1

2

Midtown Office Projects

When you visit a site to take photographs, it is wise to know beforehand if the view is going to be a ground-level or a slightly higher viewpoint. From the ground level cars and trucks can be an interference. Therefore, if you are contemplating such a view, you might even want to try a weekend for the site photos. However, most buildings will be empty on weekends, eliminating any possible higher views.

In the daytime views can be obtained from some buildings, and this will allow you to capture some activity in the street. In any case, the site comes first since it is the most difficult to manage. If site coordination is important, the point from which you take the site photos will more or less dictate the angle from which you will have to shoot the model.

However, if you should find that the model and site do not coincide precisely as planned, all is not lost. Certain perspective controls are available to the professional architectural photographer. These same controls are also available to you even with limited equipment. Perspective distortion can be overcome by simply turning the projector or enlarger from true perpendicular. Thus you can alter the perspective in either direction, horizontal or vertical, until the projected image fits your requirements. Since the building is the main subject, you will want to keep its perspective lines accurate. The site or adjoining buildings on either side can then be adjusted to coincide with the building.

When both the site and building have been projected onto the same working surface, find the vanishing points by tracing to convergence lines from the building. After this is done, all lines on the site or adjacent buildings should be drawn to fit exactly the perspective lines of the project.

4

6

3

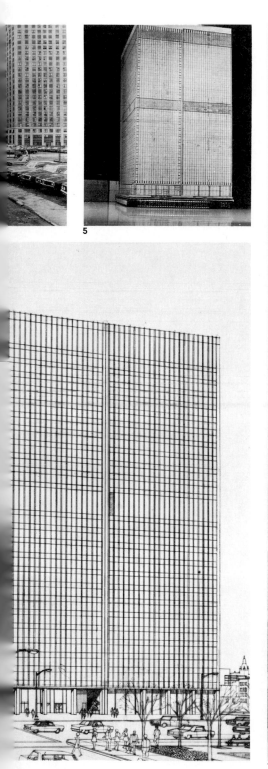

5

7

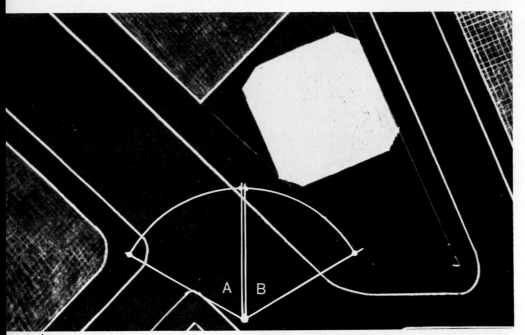

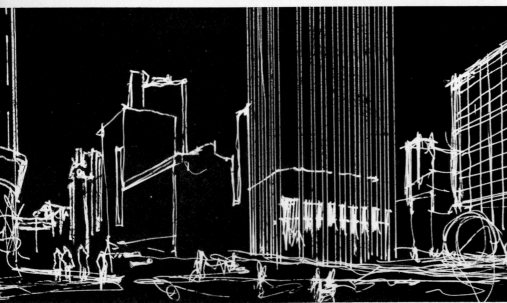

Crocker Plaza

Let the site photo create the important reference material: vanishing points, horizon line, and the shape of your project in perspective. Something from the site photo, such as people or light standards, can give you a clue as to the actual scale at any point, or you could make notes while on the site as to certain heights of adjacent structures by either measurements or estimation. From the site photo itself, there will be many checkpoints to give you aid in coordinating it with your model. The horizon line is established where the lines converge. Take the negative of the site or a proof of the negative and trace, with a pen on acetate, an outline of the shape of the projected building—a simplified outline that shows only the shape of the new proposed structure, the eye level (horizon line), and some converging lines to each vanishing point. Cut this down to the size of your camera's ground glass.

This acetate outline must lie flat against the ground glass so that the camera image will not be distorted or obscured. In most reflex cameras the acetate must be put in backwards, as the ground-glass image is reversed by the mirror inside.

With the acetate in the camera, position the camera above the plan or model which has the horizon or eye level drawn on it so that the diminishing lines and horizon lines coincide with the lines on the piece of acetate. Other lines or target points can be included for extra accuracy. Keep moving the camera around the model until a series of pictures has been taken all around the target area. This is to ensure a more accurate selection of views. If the project is a tall office tower, the top will be outside the normal 45-degree cone of vision, which would necessitate tipping the camera to include the top (4). If the camera were moved back far enough to include the top of the building within the 45-degree cone of vision without tipping the camera, it would not be coordinated with the site, unless you had planned a distant view (5).

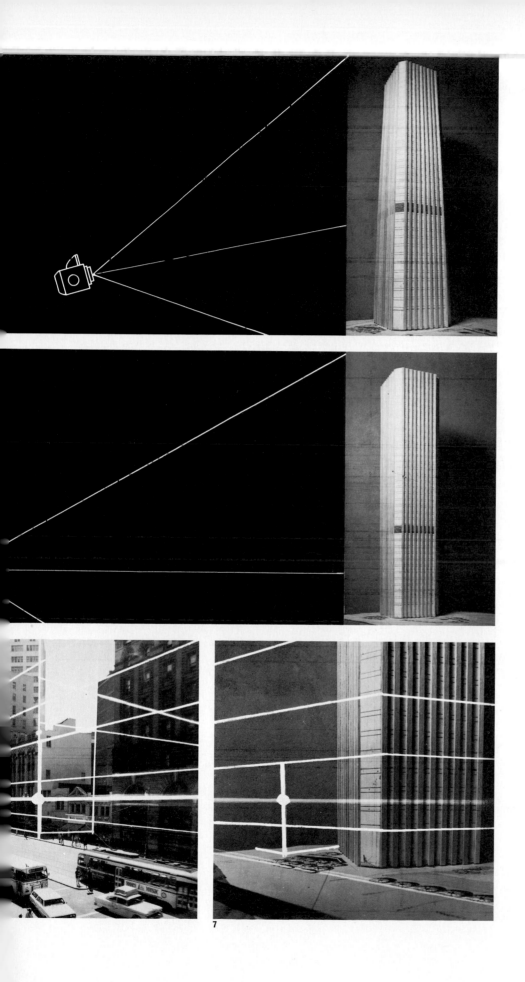

7

Crocker Plaza

Here, the station point was very close to the site, making a wide-angle perspective necessary. However, the model was photographed from the close station point and the resultant photo can be seen to include about a 45-degree angle of view (6,7).

A quick sketch on acetate (8) can determine the results of this exercise. In one instance, it was found that the ground-level view did not show the proposed structure's base or its relationship to the triangular-shaped site. The choice of view was one three stories more or less higher than the street-level view. This showed more activity on the street and a better view of the base of the structure (9).

After determining floor-to-floor heights from the model, these can be translated upward to the full height of the building; then using the vanishing points found from the site photo, the layout can be finished.

8

9

10

E. BURDEN 73

Serramonte

If you were asked to render a 900-acre community subdivision and coordinate it with all existing features of an aerial photograph, you would certainly look to the camera for assistance. Here the photographic system makes short work of an extremely complex layout problem.

To begin, you would make an outline drawing of the shape of the property by tracing it from the aerial photograph at hand. This shape is then cut out of paper and pasted over the property area. Tape this prepared site photograph to a wall and take a picture of it, letting the site area fill up the entire frame. When you get the negative developed, the property will be very clearly outlined.

Next, make a tracing of the property outline on a piece of acetate and trim it down to the size of the negative. Place this acetate in the view finder of the camera. This diagram represents the exact shape of the property recorded on the aerial photographer's camera, from his aerial station point (2).

To find the same station point in relationship to the plane in front of you is relatively simple. With the acetate outline placed on the ground glass, maneuver the camera around until the shapes line up. When all the lines of the acetate diagram line up with those of the plan, take the picture. You have just photographed the plan from the same station point as the aerial photographer who initially took the picture of the site. The rest is easy. Project the negative up until the shape fits the property outline already established, and trace the image onto paper. From here a rough sketch can give an approximation of the shape and size of the new structures. If the site is not flat, assume the plane of the photographed plan to be at some fixed ground elevation and project vertically upward on down from this plane. At this scale, measurements must be in terms of 10 feet or more, since anything less would be inconsequential.

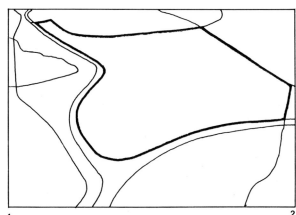

1   2

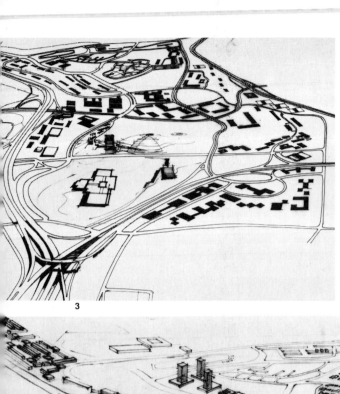

3

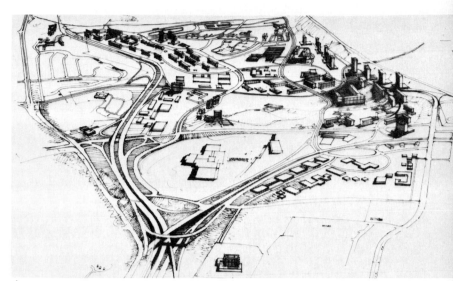

4

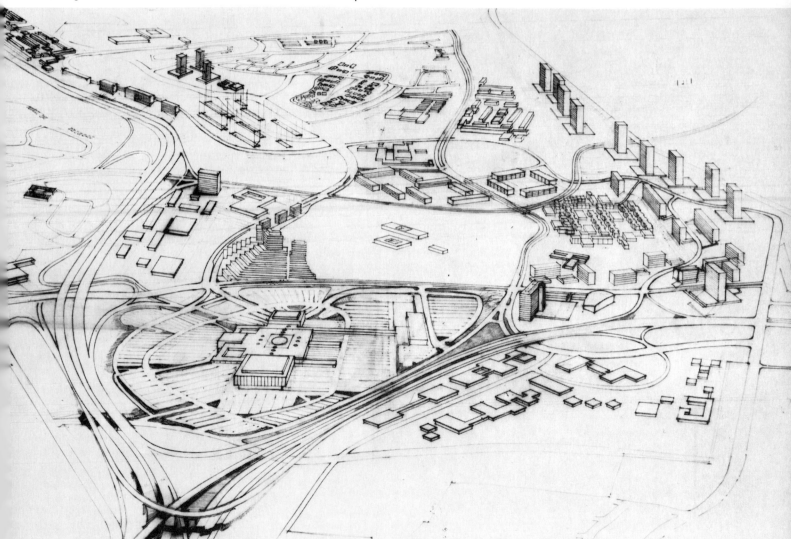

5

Serramonte

The layout can then be carried out as a separate drawing. When all the basic elements are in, the whole project is rendered with values which emulate the values in the actual aerial photograph. The rendering is then pasted over the photograph and cut out along boundaries that are natural, such as roadways and property outlines. Once set into the aerial photograph, the values can be adjusted to flow naturally from the photo to the drawing. The benefits of this photodrawing are easy to recognize. Of equal importance, however, is the experience of being able to produce a realistic representation of a project as it would look upon completion.

6

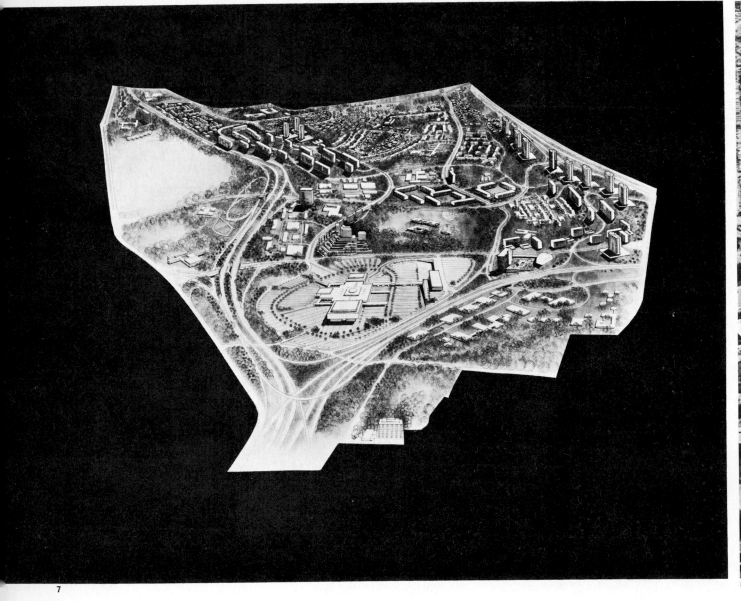

7

8

1

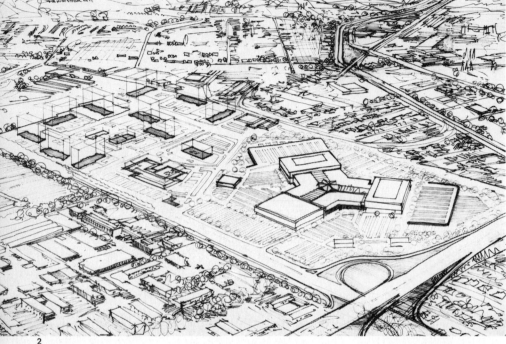

2

3

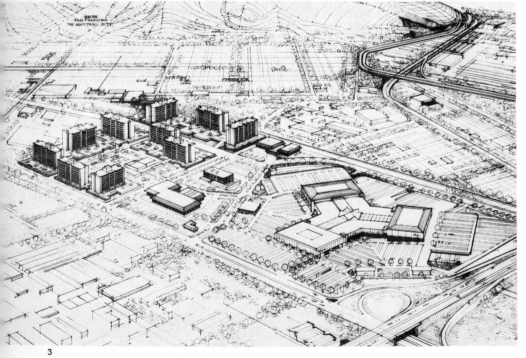

Tanforan

An aerial layout can be prepared from a photograph of the site, a photograph of a plan, a photograph of a model, or a combination of all three. The aerial photograph would dictate the angle and height from which you would photograph the plan or model. By looking at the shape of the property on the site photo, you can get an approximate idea of where you must be with the camera in order to duplicate this same viewpoint.

If you take several photographs around this general area, one will probably be close enough to work with. In this instance, exact site coordination is not entirely necessary, so this method of approximating the same relative station point as the aerial photograph is sufficient.

The photograph of the plan is projected up to the size and scale of the aerial photograph. A vertical scale can be determined from the model or by other means described earlier. This vertical scale plus the shape of the apartment tower in plan is all that is necessary to begin the layout. The model, as shown, is more complete, and all that is required is to trace the shape (1,2).

The background and foreground are obtained from the aerial photograph and the vanishing points determined from this photo. Each vanishing point must be located on the horizon line, and due to the irregularly shaped patterns of development around the project, more than 12 vanishing points are required (3).

4

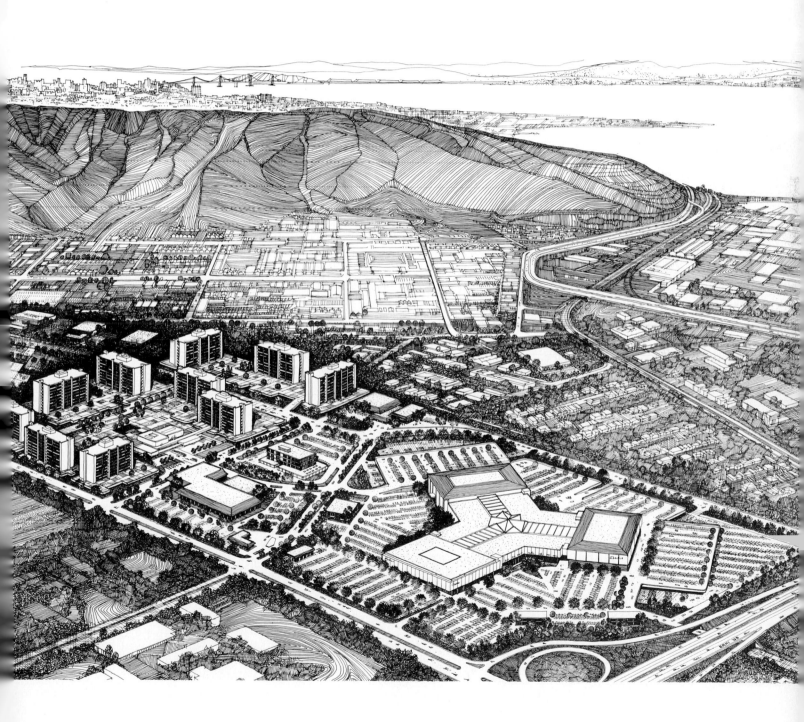

Omnitron

You may discover that a client, such as a board of regents of a university, would like to see your project in a totally realistic setting. This could be accomplished by using a technique called "photodrawing." This is a technique whereby photography is used to establish a scene. Descriptive information is then added to the photograph and the composite picture is then rephotographed. It is an actual representation which is comprehensible by anyone, and its realistic appearance is generally quite convincing.

Everything is dictated by the original photograph, as this will be the basis for the drawing.

In the project shown here, the aerial photograph (1) was taken by a photographer working for the university. The model was also built by the university. The picture of the model (2) was taken by another photographer, and it is not known whether he attempted to coordinate his model photograph with the site. However, upon first examination of the photos, it seemed as if they were taken from the identical location. So each picture was enlarged to the same size and a rough outline was made of each to see how closely they coincided (3). It was decided that they were close enough for the purposes of the rendering. A rough layout of details of the proposed structure was added to this sketchy drawing. Then the final drawing was

1

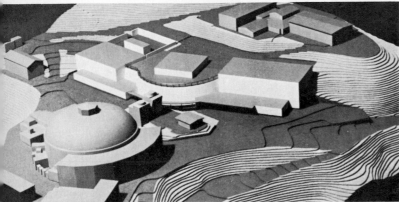

2

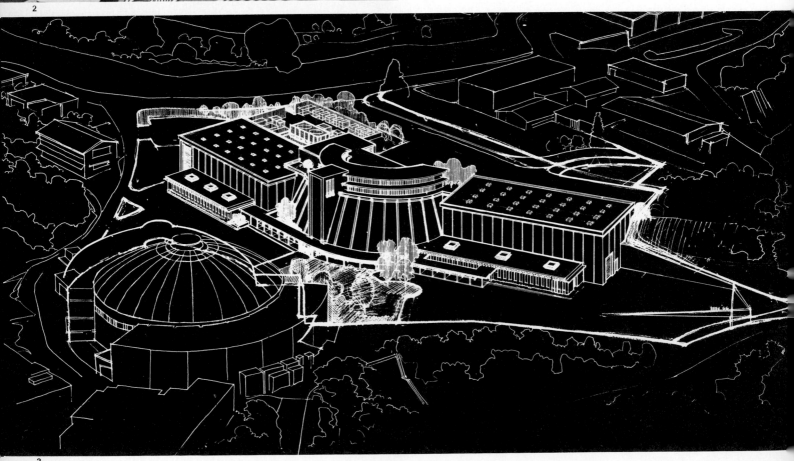

3

prepared on a separate tracing paper overlay, executed in ink line only (4). This tracing was then sent to a photographer who made an enlargement up to the size of the original photograph. The print was made on a heavy-weight mat paper, similar to the thickness of the original site photograph, which (incidentally) was in color. The print of the building was lightly pasted over the site photo with rubber cement and the print cut along outlines that followed natural boundaries such as roads, fences, and building lines. By cutting the two prints at the same time, you will assure a very close fit. The portion of the site photo to be replaced by the rendering was then lifted out and the rendering pasted in its place.

Color and tonal values were then added to the building with ink, pastel, or colored pencil. The colors were matched as closely as possible to the site photo to heighten the effect of realism.

When the drawing was completed in color, there was still a difference in surface texture of the two parts of the drawing. The color photograph of the site, although a mat surface, was glossier than the rendering that was set in. This was overcome by spraying the entire drawing with a mat finish. It could have been sprayed glossy, but the softness of the colors looked better in a mat finish. The entire drawing was later rephotographed on color film and used for reproduction.

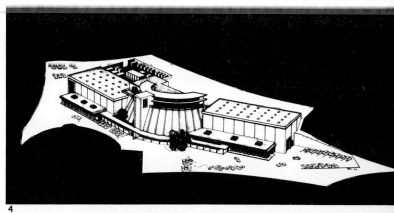

4

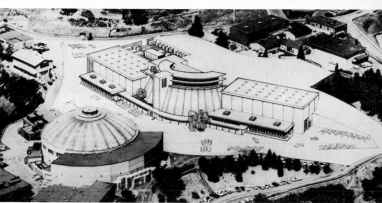

5

6

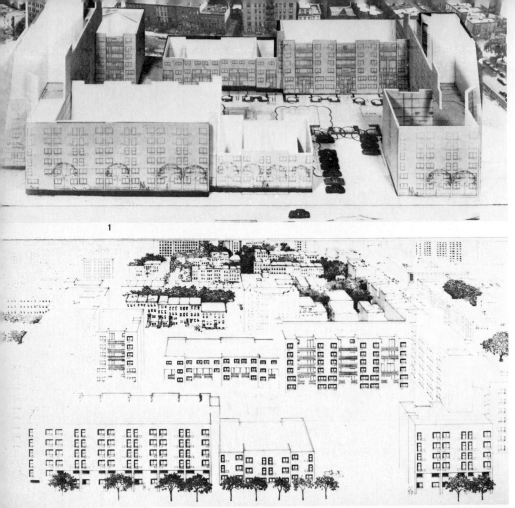

1

Middle-Income Apartments

These two apartment-house projects utilize similar techniques in nearly every detail. Each uses a styrofoam cardboard model with the building elevations pasted on the sides facing the camera. Each is incomplete in the roof area to permit a true picture of the other side of the building. Each features an inner courtyard, so a low-angle aerial vantage point was used to show a portion of the inner walls. The background in each case was created from photographing the site, although here the techniques differ slightly.

In the first case, the only accessible vantage point was the roof of a nearby apartment building (1). The architect for the project had taken a series of snapshots and included them with the plans for the rendering. They were assembled into a sort of overlapping mosaic. Although the perspective curved away from the viewer on each end, it was fairly accurate toward the center (2). The

2

3

true height, scale, and window detail could then be interpreted in the layout stage so that they closely resemble the actual background (3).

In the second case (4), the background was also taken separately, but on one negative. The background here was a distant view of the Manhattan skyline. The site was only blocks from the river, yet the city skyline was not totally visible because of the obstruction of nearby buildings. So two pictures were combined (4); one taken at the edge of the Hudson River and one taken at the far edge of the site from an elevated railroad trestle.

Once the layouts were completed, the similarity ended. The first drawing (3) was executed in black and white with ink line drawing. Tones were done with airbrush. The second one (5) was rendered in full color using colored markers, colored pencils, and opaque tempera for the highlights.

4

5

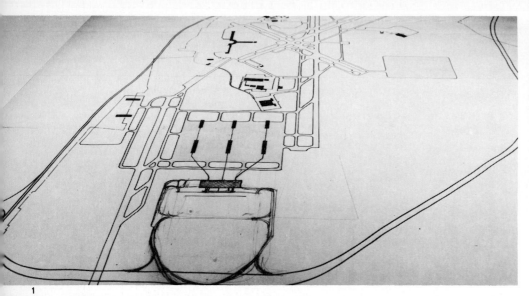

1

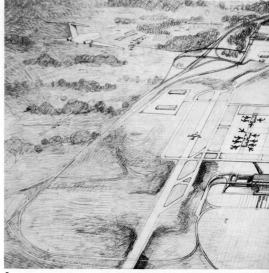

2

Greater Pittsburgh Airport

The aerial vantage point could have no more appropriate use than in depicting an airport. If you were attempting to show a single large structure, you might choose an aerial station point. And if you decided to show the entire airport, you would have no other choice. In the example shown here, all that was necessary was to photograph the plan of the runway pattern. The structures were insignificantly small by comparison, and could be laid out from this photograph of the plan.

First a series of photos were taken from many angles and from different heights. The one most appealing put the station point nearly perpendicular to the main pattern of structures and nearly parallel to the main takeoff and landing runways.

This view was enlarged and a pencil layout was executed, roughing in all the structures. Airplanes were included in the layout to dramatize the sense of the aerial approach and to provide scale. This was accomplished by photographing a plastic model airplane. The model plane was attached to a tripod, positioned in space, and photographed in different attitudes in relation to the plan. The one selected for the rendering was meant to give the impression of a plane preparing to land. Without the plane the rendering would have lacked scale. With this problem solved by an inexpensive toy and the camera, the rest of the rendering went smoothly.

3

4

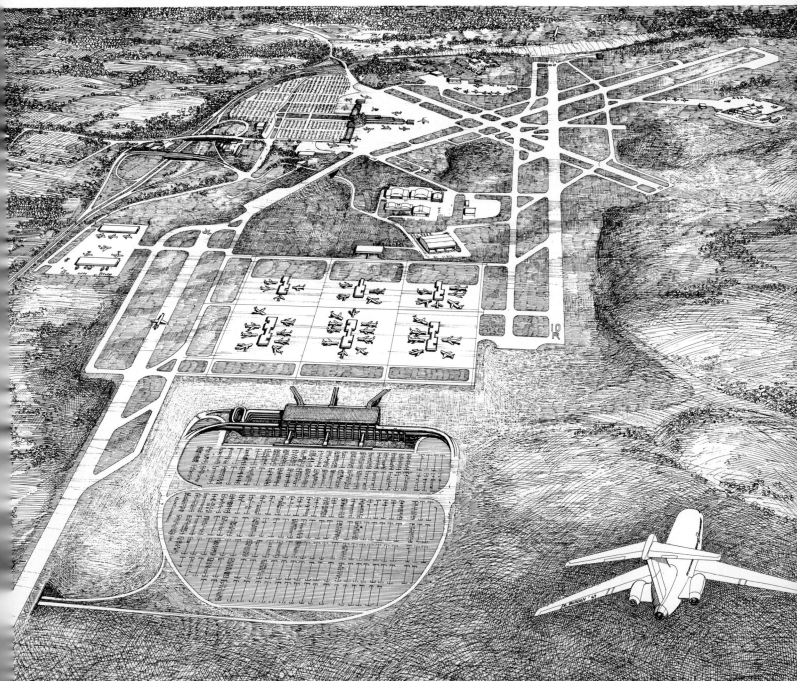

1

Pan Am Terminal

The photographic process takes on a new meaning and a new dimension when one is confronted with increasingly more complex problems such as this airport rendering. The problem was to illustrate an addition to an existing facility within the complex of a major international airport. The first clue to a solution was offered by a construction photograph of the existing terminal. Since the composition and angle of view was appropriate to show the new expansion, it was used as a basis from which to photograph the new addition. The camera was positioned high above the model until the image of the model lined up with the acetate outline in the camera viewer. The elliptical terminal building provided an excellent point of reference. Then each of the two pictures, the site photo and the model photo, was enlarged to the same scale. The model picture was cut out and pasted over the site photo in position. This composite picture was then rephotographed and enlarged onto mylar chronaflex instead of paper, yielding a transparent medium on which to work (1,2,3).

The chronoflex photograph was thereafter scratched with an X-acto knife, which yielded a texture in reverse. The purpose was to build up ink textures approaching the values of a photograph and to break down the value quality of the photograph to imitate a drawing. When the two textures merged, the result was a photodrawing, neither photograph nor drawing but containing the best of each. In the final drawing the textures blended together so well that it was difficult to tell where the photograph ended and the drawing began (5).

2

3

4

5

1

SECOND AVENUE

2

3

Phipps Plaza

If you cannot find a stock picture, you will have to have the site flown over either by an aerial photographer, by a regular photographer and a helicopter, or by yourself as the last resort. See pages 24–25 for tips on aerial surveys.

The model was constructed of styrofoam board on which the building elevations were pasted, using rubber cement (1). These elevations were very helpful since they com-

pletely eliminated the need for elaborate measuring and scaling (2). The layout was drawn in ink on matte acetate and the background was drawn in pencil. This original was photographed and color was applied to the print with colored pencil. The background was kept softer in tone, texture, and color to focus attention on the project. (See pages 102–103 for the final color drawing.)

Drawings by: Ernest Burden

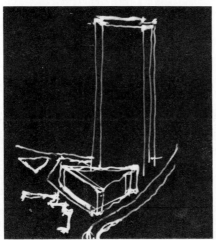

New York
Telephone Building

Aerial renderings can be difficult to plan because they show so much of the surroundings (1). Therefore, special techniques are needed to focus attention on the building and still show the building in its actual environment. If you have only one aerial photograph, the viewpoint is dictated.

However, if you have a number of photographs to choose from, you can select the best view. All you need for this study is a rough model (2). By sketching the approximate view you want on acetate and putting it in the ground glass of the camera, you can take any number of views at the same time (3). Then enlarge the model to the right size, cut out the outline, and paste it over the aerial photo (4).

In this study it was apparent that the background overshadowed the building. Therefore, the angle chosen for the drawing turned out to be a high oblique view extremely close to the site. This view also foreshortened the height of the 60-story tower so it would not look so ominous within the existing neighborhood.

1

2   3

4

5

1

3

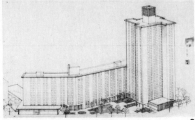

2

Model Cities Apartments

The earliest stage of exploration and study for an aerial drawing might be photographs of a simple block model, or mass model. This approach gets the photographic process started and provides a realistic base to make your choice of view.

Once you have selected the aerial photograph, the rest of the decisions are set. You now have to make everything fit down to the smallest detail. Fitting the photograph of the mass model to the aerial photograph is a simple matter of following the techniques described on page 104.

A simple tracing of the outlines of the model (1, 2) will get you started on the layout. Next the windows and other details can be added (3, 4). Once the layout is complete, paste it over the aerial photo. Matte acetate is the best surface for tracing over the combined picture.

Now you can devote more time to the rendering technique itself. For aerial renderings, the background is as important as the building since it cannot be ignored as in a ground-level drawing. Here, each project was rendered fully in ink (5, 6), including the background. The technique used for the background was a free-hand sketch style to set it apart from the hard ink-line treatment of the building.

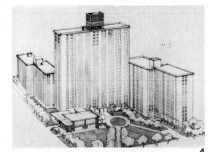

4

5

6

Convention Center

Once you are accomplished in using the techniques of aerial layouts, you can concentrate on methods of representing the background and rendering the building.

Here are two examples, with differing techniques, although both were drawn on matte acetate. In the Miami Convention Center, the low buildings were sketched in a freehand style with ink. The building was drawn and textured with ink line and cross-hatch (1). The roof of the convention center was toned by drawing a cross-hatched texture and then scratching it with thin strokes with an Exacto knife (2). Using this technique, you can approach the soft tonal quality of a shaded pencil drawing using a hard ink line as the base.

Apartment Towers

In the aerial drawing of the apartment building, the difference is in the background treatment and the shading on the building. The matte acetate is a fairly good surface for drawing with wax-based pencils, such as Prismacolor black. Once the ink outlines were drawn, the rest of the shading was done using the black colored pencil. Buildings in the background were drawn in pencil only (3). Eliminating the outlines on the background buildings produced a much softer effect in contrast with the crisp lines of the new apartment tower (4).

3

4

2

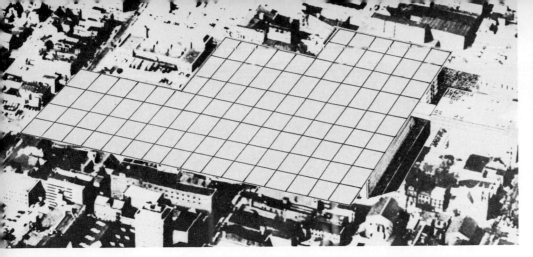

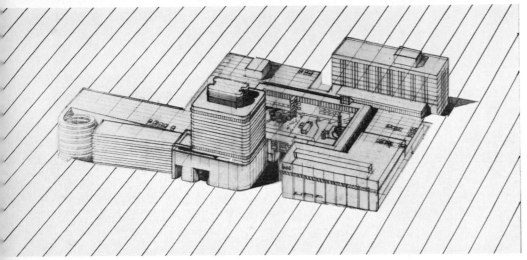

Lancaster Square

Any project in an urban environment that lends itself to a photodrawing technique has many built-in guidelines. Streets are generally at right angles and all vanishing points can be taken directly from the aerial photo. One side will usually have a sharper vanishing point than the other. In the case of the distant vanishing point, you can set up a custom grid to guide you in drawing converging lines. Heights can be taken directly from adjacent buildings.

The rough layout, after all these things are taken into account, is prepared on tracing paper. The final drawing is executed from the layout then photographed and enlarged or reduced to fit into the aerial photo.

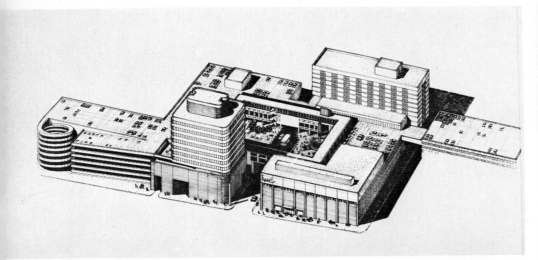

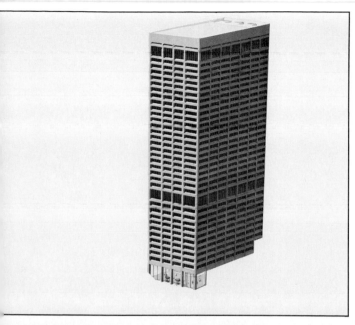

One Beacon Street

Rarely does one get a clear view of a total building even in an aerial. In the case here the site was in a relatively tight, restricted street in Boston. A ground-level viewpoint would have been pointless. In addition, it would not have shown the relationships of the new structure to several architecturally important new projects in that area.

The building was simply rendered separately, in tempera, so that the values of the set-in building matched the values of the black and white photograph. The final composite drawing was completed by placing a photograph of the rendered building directly into the aerial photo and reshooting the composite.

Rendering by: Rudolph Associates
Superimposition by: Jack Horner
Pennyroyal

1

U.S.S.R./U.N. Mission

One of the quickest ways to study a proposed project in an existing setting is to take an aerial photograph and sketch in the new buildings on an overlay. The pencil is the best technique for this kind of drawing. The wide tonal range from white to black makes it easier to match the values of the photograph.

In this instance, two opposite views were chosen to illustrate a new apartment complex atop a prominent hill (1, 3). The layouts were done directly over the aerials. The drawing was then completed by using pencil on paper. The finished drawings of the buildings were then cut out around the outlines and pasted over the aerial photograph.

Final tones were then added to blend the drawing into the aerial photograph (2, 4). By keeping the same relative tonal values and sun angle, a sense of realism can be achieved from a simple pencil-sketch technique.

Drawings by: Robert Fisher

2　　　　　　　　　　　　　4

3

Urban Shopping Complex

There are usually stock aerial photos of important areas such as this major shopping-center district not far from New York City (1). The purpose was to study a new major shopping center within the existing complex. One simple box model was all that was required to produce the series of studies. Using the acetate-diagram-in-the-ground-glass technique (2), each view was quickly recorded, and the resulting negatives were checked to see how they aligned with the diagram. Prints of the model were pasted over the aerial photos (3, 4) in the proper alignment and rephotographed for the final prints.

Photos by: Ernest Burden

1

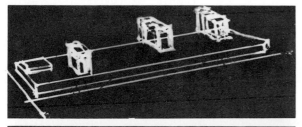

2

3

4

East Point

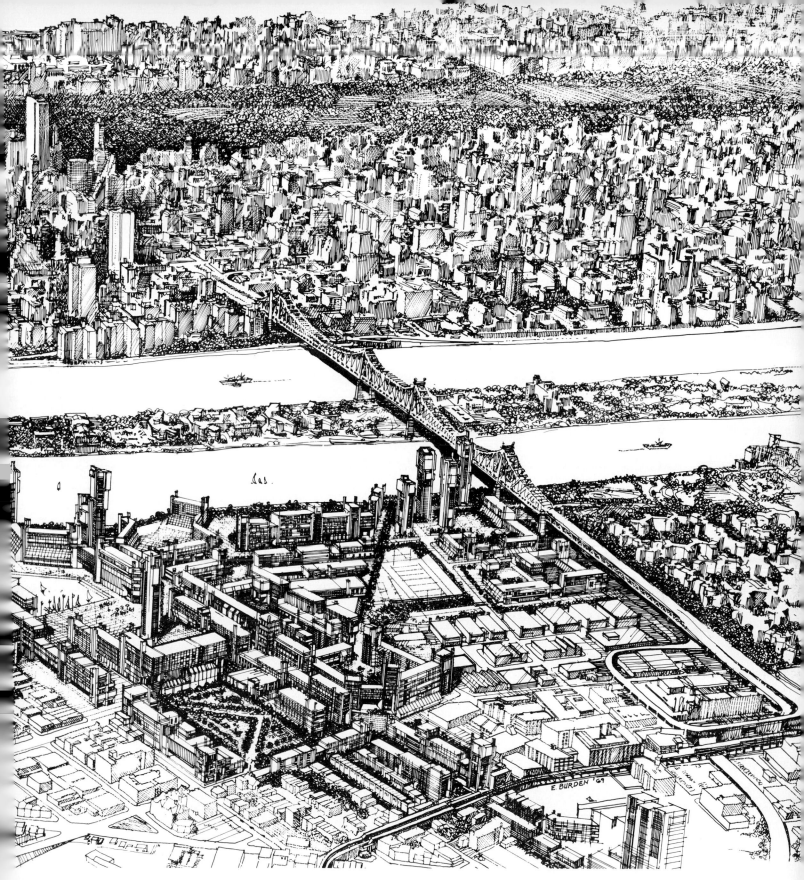

E. BURDEN '69

A partial cityscape may present many problems, but foremost of these would be the decisions of how to begin and when to end the drawing.

The basis for any drawing of this scope will most often be an aerial photograph. To determine how to end the drawing, consider the problems involved in the area of your new project and its relationship to the rest of the drawing. Then consider the limit of the drawing, in relationship to these considerations. You will have to begin the drawing from the aerial photograph. Careful examination of the picture will show that it is a three-point perspective.

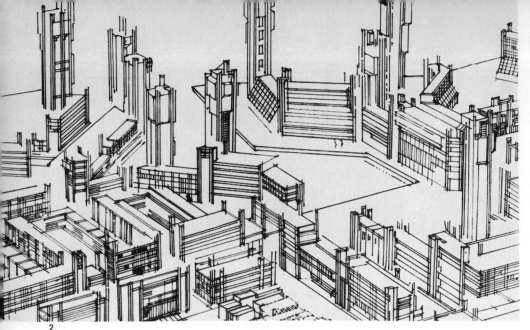

2

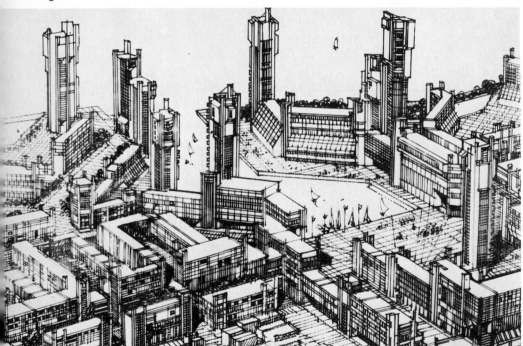

3

East Point

If you draw a line parallel to the images on the extreme left and another line parallel to the images on the extreme right, you will discover that each one will be 5 to 10 degrees off from true vertical, which should appear in the center of the picture.

Using the principle of the custom grid, turned vertically, you can establish the true vanishing point in the third dimension. Unless this is followed, the entire picture will look unnatural. All other vanishing points can be determined directly from the aerial photograph. They will be very far away, resulting in an isometric type of projection. Any sort of grid can be established in plan view, using the existing street patterns to determine where new buildings will go. The entire layout of the plan of the new project should be placed over the aerial first to ensure correct alignment. After this is satisfactory, use the third vanishing point grid to construct the verticals.

Since most redevelopment projects precede actual architectural design by years, you may find some need to let technique become design. Actual floor heights are simply lines, balconies, and projections; window divisions and solids can be created while you draw. Carefully controlled textures can give the impression of architectural elements. For the existing city in the background a looser, sketchy style is used to offer contrast to the crispness of the new development. Here again technique becomes design as dots, strokes, and shading represent an encompassing view of a metropolitan area.

4

5

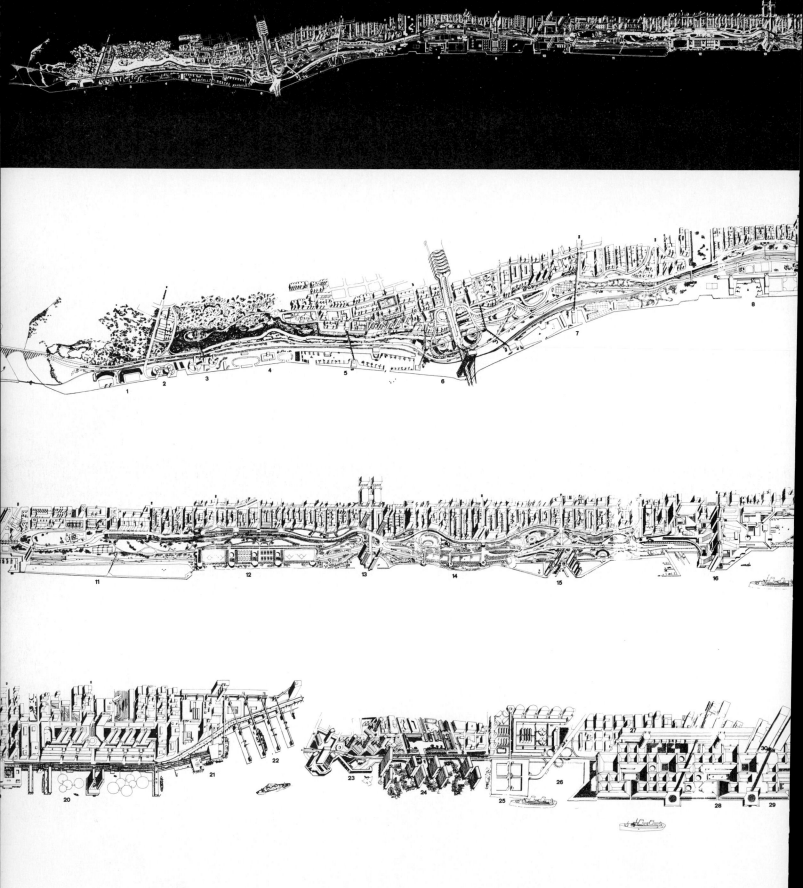

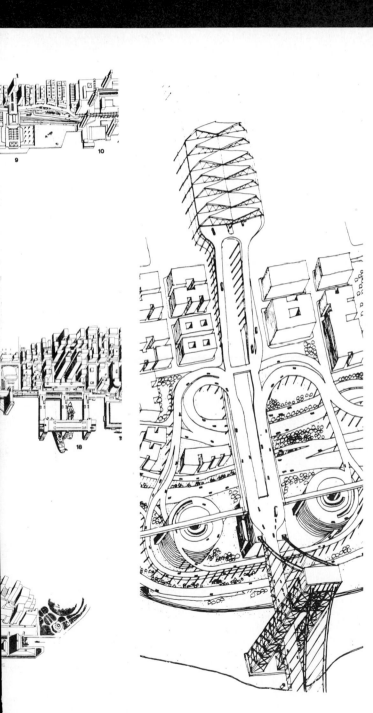

Hudson River Project

Here is the aerial layout carried to its ultimate conclusion: A true isometric drawing based on a pure orthographic plan. This drawing of the entire Hudson Riverfront portion of Manhattan was undertaken by six teams of architects, planners, and architecture students as a total conceptual design of two major arterial traffic ways. One was the Hudson River and its function, and the second the Westside Highway bordering the island of Manhattan. The source for the drawing was the city block maps upon which some new design ideas were incorporated.

The actual drawing was executed by three teams of designers. Therefore, It was imperative to establish certain design and rendering criteria before commencing. Each office worked on its own portion of the drawing. A basic technique was established whereby a standard angle for the isometric projection and a standard vertical scale were settled on.

The actual drawing was over 50 feet long, each section being about 15 feet or more. Since it could never be reproduced at that size, a very loose, almost cartoon style of drawing was agreed upon, to be followed by a joint effort on the actual work.

Even though the drawing was produced by over 50 different people, it has a remarkable coherency. This is the direct result of careful examination of the problems of presenting a project of such enormous scope, then determining the proper solution.

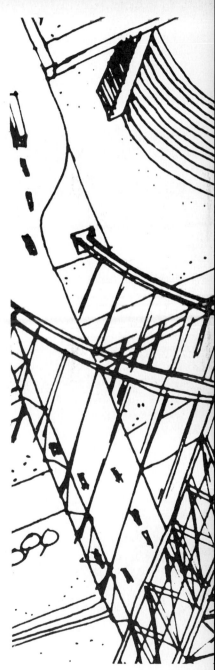

Cityscapes

Cityscapes, whether partial or more inclusive views, demand rendering layout and technique of an entirely different nature than the single building. It is a layout of many little parts, each one no different from an actual rendering of the same building except for scale. In an aerial rendering of a single building, attention is paid to detail of the building. In the cityscape, the detail is the building. In the layout you must follow all the natural perspective and convergence of the aerial photograph, or it will look peculiar.

Try to look for compositional devices, major arterial highways, lakes, rivers, or bridges. Also try to minimize all detail in the extreme background, foreground, and if possible on each side. This will keep the focus of attention in the center of the drawing. This can be accomplished by keeping edges of the drawing sketchier than the inside portions. However, do not be too concerned with a literal translation of the city itself but look for design elements to add interest to it as a drawing; otherwise the actual aerial photo may be of more use.

1

2

3

Value Studies

The best technique for any drawing is the result of many factors. The most important one to study is value: where to place the focus, how to lead the eye to the center of interest, and how to balance the drawing with lights and darks. This series of value studies by Ron Love illustrates how important it is to study the final outcome of the drawing in sketch form.

Drawings by: Ron Love

4

5

6

Steve Oles

In choosing a medium to accommodate and convey his own concept of reality in an architectural rendering, Steve Oles was attracted to the use of pencil. The pencil allows a maximum range of expression through tonal values. Ease of control, predictability, and variability of texture were equally important considerations.

The pencil used to produce the drawing shown here was of the wax-base type rather than the graphite or carbon pencil. These latter two tend to smudge easily, and the graphite will produce a reflective surface when heavily applied. It is also difficult to get an intense black with a graphite pencil.

These are all important considerations in attempting to produce renderings which have a quality of freshness and high degree of consistency.

Lawrence Perron

Here the pencil takes on a new dimension. If used by itself, it will produce effects of light and shade by varying the intensities or directions of the stroke of the pencil.

If the same drawing were done on a board that had previously been prepared with gesso, the result would be a combination of the pencil strokes and the prearranged texture of the gesso. This combination, when used successfully, gives a spontaneous quality to the drawing.

In the past, the pencil delineator could rely on the detailing of the building for interest in his drawing. Today, however, new techniques must be evolved to appropriately depict the architectural forms of today.

Drawing by: Jack Barkley

146

Community Federal Center

A simple ink-line rendition of a building can be very effective. The values can then be controlled, as was done so skillfully here. The surrounding entourage was handled in the same manner, using a minimum of lines to define the forms and provide the shading.

Kent Memorial Library

This drawing displays an extreme amount of control and careful balancing of tonal qualities. Shadow areas are not too dark, and the general quality of filtered and reflected light is very skillfully handled. All tones are built up from overlapping textures which are all very carefully studied and controlled. The interior courtyard is handled very effectively by showing a central ornamental tree in light tones against a darker interior. The total cohesiveness of this drawing was achieved by the careful relationships of the textures.

Drawing by: J. Henderson Barr

To capture the quality of the relaxed environment necessary for reading books, a soft pencil technique was used for this interior. The entire room was entourage with walls of books substituting for a hard architectural treatment.

Each reading area had a windowed view of the garden court through which light would filter in. The extremely delicate shading and absence of ruled lines adds to the softness of the effect. Sunlight was further emphasized by rendering the tree in the courtyard in strong highlight tones, again avoiding linear definition or harsh shadows.

Gamal ElZoghby

In this aerial view of a city square the board was not prepared with gesso. The buildings were all outlined freehand in ink and then some general tones were applied with charcoal. Finally shades and shadows and fine detail were put in with pencil.

The combination of media, whether it be ink, gesso, pencil, or charcoal, can result in an extremely wide range of expression.

Davis Bité

Inspiration for some of the elaborate textures that Davis developed in the evolution of his style can be traced to his admiration of engravings of the old masters. These include such masters as Gustave Doré, Piranesi, and Bibienna. He then developed the style of using a carefully controlled overlapping of lines to produce the values he wants.

However, even the most carefully studied area still has an element of freshness to it which comes from his very bold use of the ink line.

Considerations of light and shade and of reflected light were all carefully balanced, yet the total effect of this technique is still one of spontaneity.

Brian Burr

Interior spaces are more difficult to portray in terms of the quality of light, which usually comes from an artificial light source. However, today many of our greatest interior spaces are atriums covered by vast tubular-frame skylights. So you have in effect an interior space with exterior lighting. Brian Burr's solution was to use the skylight as a diffuser of the light, spreading it evenly throughout the vast interior space. Thus he was able to show clarity and detail throughout, especially in areas within each level. The drawing is a combination of techniques using ink line, airbrush, colored markers, and colored pencils.

Davis Bité Here ink-line work is effectively combined with free-hand ink textures. The clear-cut angularity of the structures is further emphasized and enhanced by the textural treatment in the foreground and sky. The use of hatching to build up the darker values was very skillfully handled here. Certainly the architectural forms were given a new dimension by the creative use of lines.

Ron Love

The technique used in this drawing intended to show the structures by means of tonal contrast rather than by means of outline. This was achieved by the use of value changes made up primarily of cross-hatching and stippling. To control these tonal changes, they were all worked out beforehand in pencil and then drawn in ink.

This drawing was executed primarily for reproduction purposes. This crisp linear style would yield excellent line engravings for magazine reproduction.

In order to maintain the same open quality throughout the entire drawing, the foliage was treated very loosely. This technique allowed the page to become an integral part of the drawing.

Ron Love

This type of rendering is approached as a regular watercolor rendering rather than as an ink drawing with a wash of color over it. The entire value pattern and color are worked out in advance, much the same as in a tempera rendering. The line drawing is done on watercolor board using waterproof ink. The color is then applied using various methods of masking, much like an airbrush drawing.

Walter Thomason

The entire area of a prominent urban square in downtown San Francisco was used to provide an elegant setting for a new Saks Fifth Avenue store. The technique of using pencil on vellum is perhaps the most predictable of all mediums. Tonal values can be built up. They can also be erased or held back. Since the entire drawing can be worked on in these subtle stages, the exact value desired can be reached.

Brian Burr

Another method of building up the tonal values of a drawing can be seen here. The ink-line work and textures for the entire drawing were carried to completion first. Trees were completely rendered and the grass textures put in. Materials were all carefully rendered on the structures and all the values put in with line work.

Then the drawing was masked area by area and additional values were put in by spraying the unmasked area with ink in an airbrush. The tones applied were kept necessarily light because the values had already been carried so far in the ink drawing underneath. After each of the several areas had been sprayed, the sky tone was put in.

Marc Nisbet

All three of these projects demonstrate Nisbet's technique for highlighting and emphasizing the structure. He utilizes a dark paper background upon which he builds up lighter tones, using Prismacolor pencils and, in some cases, opaque tempera. The result is a nicely modulated appearance with brilliant highlights, typical of the lighting conditions in Middle Eastern projects. **Drawings by: Marc Nisbet**

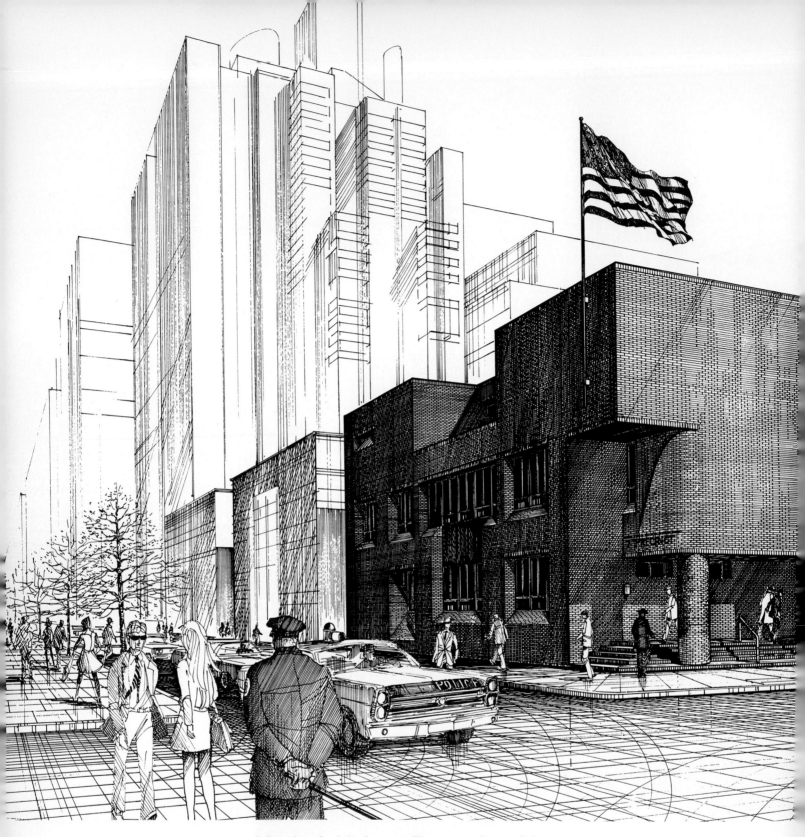

Mark deNalovy-Rozvadovski

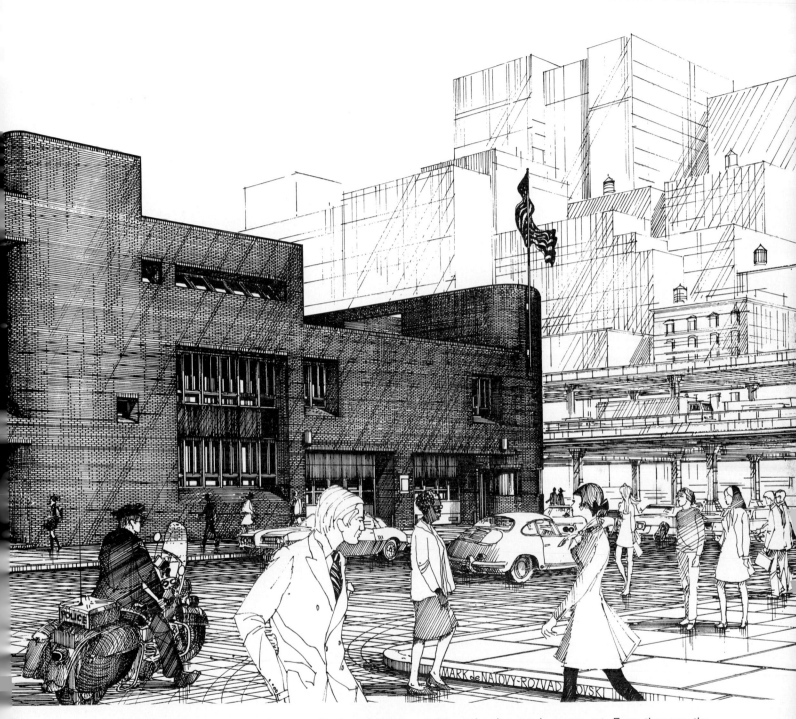

Following a pencil layout done on the board, Mark begins to draw in the entourage in ink. This gives a freshness and spontaneity to the figures and keeps them light and airy. It also strengthens the suggestion of movement. After the entourage is drawn in ink, work is begun on the structure. As soon as the entire building is outlined, all the pencil is removed, and from that point on the drawing becomes art. From then on, the entire drawing is worked up to completion all at once. This allows it to be treated as a total composition. In each case the building is rendered as a solid object, and the rest of the drawing supports the composition. By treating the ground plane and the figures lightly, the effect of movement is maintained.

J. Henderson Barr

This drawing was executed on transparent mylar, drawn directly over a very carefully detailed line drawing underlay. All the final drawing was done freehand, to avoid harsh sharp lines. The technique used was short, small strokes using a black wax-based pencil. Using this technique, the lightest tones in the drawing are put in first, and then these are gradually built up to the darkest values.

Lincoln Plaza Ernest Burden Ink line on acetate

1

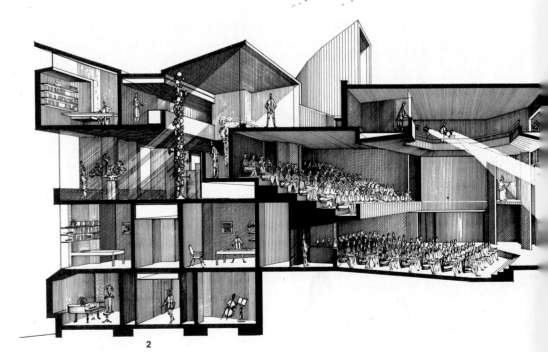

2

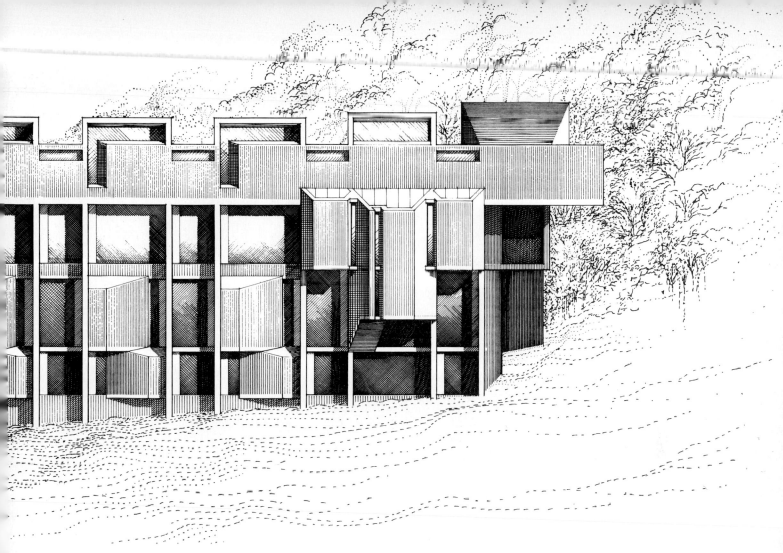

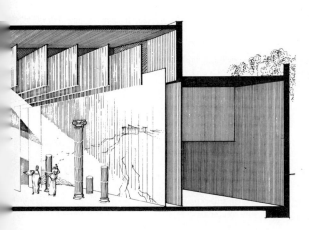

Here a rendering technique is used to render an elevation and section. Usually drawings of this nature are done extremely large and the values studied in the reducing glass to be sure that they hold up at a reduced scale. The rich textures created in the interior cutaway section are produced by many layers of overlapping cross-hatching. First established by a vertical line, then by 45-degree strokes as the second direction, and then an opposite 45-degree stroke if the area still needs to be darker. And lastly, lines emanating from a station point will add additional hatching if necessary. In addition to this, the closeness of the lines can control to a great degree the value on any given area.

Davis Bité

1   2

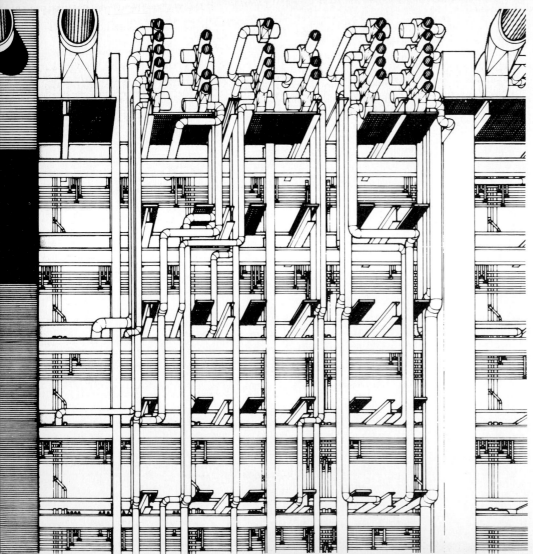

Sectional Perspectives

This laboratory building housed a series of research facilities. In order to depict the high technological functions, two sections were drawn in opposite locations within the structure (1, 3). One part of the exterior was rendered to show the close architectural relationship between the mechanical equipment and the building's exterior form. While one section emphasized the mechanical-equipment aspect (2), the other one showed more of the high-tech-

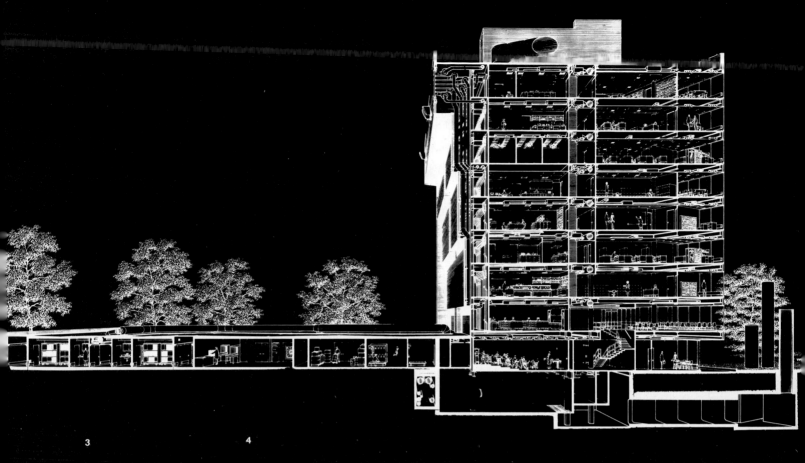

3   4

nology laboratories on each floor (4). By selecting a station point about one-third of the distance from grade to top of the struoture, David Morgan was able to draw a realistic sectional perspective without extreme distortion, since he showed activity and spaces close to the sectional cut line on the upper floor. On the lower floors, he could show more depth in the rooms, as they were closer to the eye level and would appear more normal.

Drawings by: David Morgan

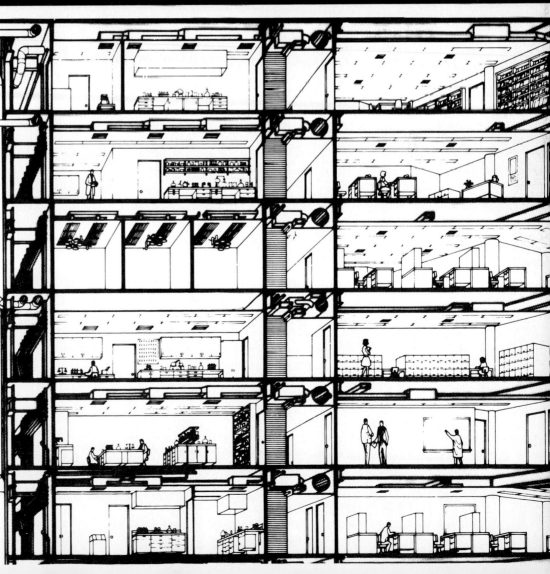

Textured Screen Prints

1

2

A straight ink-line drawing is crisp and clear (1). However, it does not have so much interest and appeal as one with a textured ink line (5). To turn an ink-line drawing into a textured one is relatively easy. In order to introduce texture in the sky, you need to start with a solid black. Then a negative is made of this drawing and printed with a screen texture, sandwiched with the negative (3).

The resulting print will have the solid ink lines interrupted by the screen, producing a soft-textured drawing. The drawing can be rendered darker by adding an ink line over the texture to intensify certain areas. The resulting drawing then retains the crispness, clarity, and exactness of the ink line but with the softening effect of the textured screen.

Drawings by: Ernest Burden

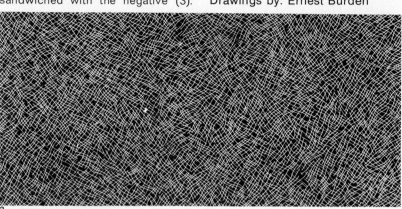

3

4

5

Gamal ElZoghby

In this drawing, the entire form was built up from specially created textural patterns. All outlines were created by placing different textures next to each other. All other lines were formed by dots and dashes.

After the drawing was completely worked out with these textures, certain portions were masked and sprayed with airbrush. These gave the opportunity to create new values by spraying some of the textures with a darker value than others.

1

Photoscreen Prints

The textured screen print can come in very handy when you want to make presentation prints of rough study models (1). Even if the model pictures have distracting back-grounds, they can still produce us-able prints. You can make a photo-graphic print using a textured screen sandwiched on top of the print paper. Put both the paper and screen under glass and make your exposure as usual. This will reduce the photographic values to the tex-ture of the screen (2). You can then add ink lines to darken areas or, in this case, to eliminate the distracting background (3).

The presentation here showed multiple views of a large project. First, the prints were made through the textured screen. Then they were assembled into the multiple-image layout and the values in each were adjusted to relate to the total compo-sition (4).

4

2

3

Photodrawings by: Ernest Burden

Hinge Block

The placement of figures and trees in this interior rendering is secondary to a device sometimes overlooked in interior views. The wide range of tonal values employed here is the feature which gives this drawing its most characteristic quality. The values of light and shade have been very carefully studied and quite consciously controlled.

In addition to the rendition of light and shade, other qualities of light are given expression here. These include reflected light from floor surfaces and filtered and diffused light from the transparent roof enclosure.

The ideal medium to express these nuances of value is the pencil. A shading range from broad dark to delicate off-white is possible with pencil. It is an extremely versatile medium useful in creating the many moods demanded in interior renderings.

Drawing by: Steve Oles

Combined Techniques

The nature of the project will sometimes dictate the technique, but usually it is the "look" or impression that one wants to create that will govern the selection. For the downtown office building (1), a soft-pencil technique on a rough illustration board was chosen to "soften" its appearance.

In the drawings of the shopping plaza (2) and courtyard (3), a combination of ink outline and pencil shading was used on a matte-surfaced acetate. The matte surface is good for ink and will take a soft Prismacolor pencil tone.
Drawings by: Ernest Burden

2

3

1

Value Delineation

In his new book, *Value Delineation*, Steve Oles writes, "The value delineation system is a conceptual approach to the realistic rendering of not-yet-existing form in light. Nature is perceived by the eye not as an array of lines, but as areas of color that translate monochromatically into tones of gray between black and white." This quality can be seen in this series for the Pennslyvania Avenue beautification project in Washington. He chose one viewpoint for both a day (1) and a nighttime (2) view. The third drawing in the series features an outdoor café (3) on the other side of the tree-lined avenue. The drawings are done on a rough illustration board using colored pencils. The texture of the board shows through in all three views.

This same technique was used on the second project, a medium-rise structure in downtown Boston. This technique is especially evident in the ground-level view (4). In the aerial view (5), the drawing was done separately and spliced into the existing aerial photograph. Oles takes great care to ensure that all the values of the new structure relate to the surroundings. This care includes, of course, attention to the precise angle of the sun and the relative shadows portrayed in the aerial photograph.

Drawings by: Steve Oles

2   3

4

5

Multiple Studies

Renderings are usually most helpful in the design-study stage. This is the perfect time to draw the building and study its form. Sometimes more than one drawing is required to study the appearance of different building materials. In the case on page 194 (1), a study was made between a dark bronze-colored glass and spandrel and a light aluminum spandrel with light glass (2). In order to make the comparison more objective, each drawing was laid out using the same viewpoint, the same group of figures, and the identical background. Although they were two completely separate drawings, the cloud pattern and the sky were both kept as close as possible for a more accurate comparison.

The project on the right required the same kind of study except that in the top pictures, the light structures were drawn against a dark sky with approximately the same cloud pattern (3, 4). In the lower two pictures, the sky was made lighter. In all other aspects, all four drawings were identical at the base and the entourage was drawn exactly the same (5, 6).

Drawings by: David Morgan

1

2

3

5

4

6

Coordinated Viewpoints

The techniques that were used so successfully in these drawings of Water Tower Place in Chicago are a combination of consistency of style and a logical coordination of viewpoints. First comes the distant view, then a closeup of the arcade leading to the entry. Finally, the lobby escalator and cascading gardens cause one's eye to leap up to an interior lobby or court leading into a main atrium area. The soft-textured tonal values are very carefully used to direct and focus attention.

Drawings by: J. Henderson Barr

196

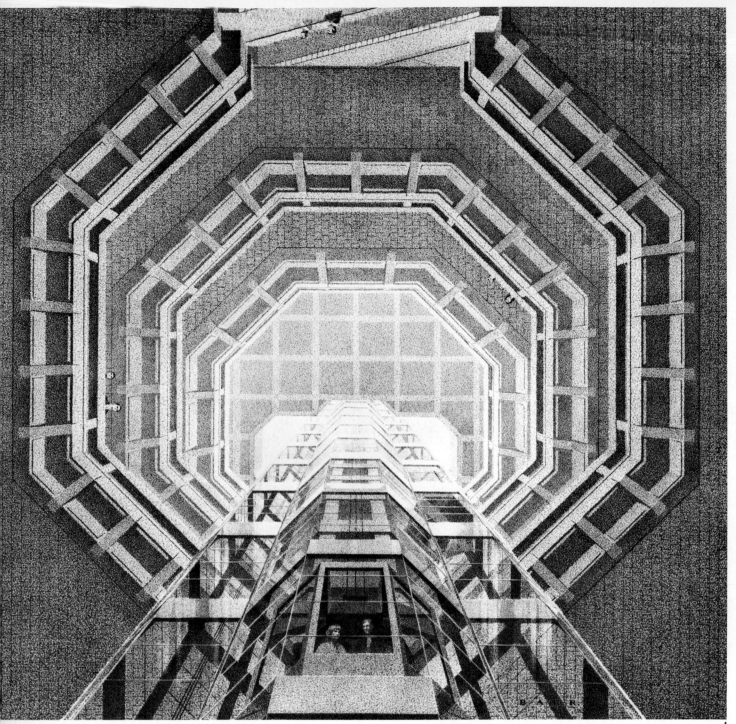

Water Tower Place

The atrium in Water Tower Place is the main attraction of the building, and the two drawings here make that apparent. The sectional perspective (2) is cut exactly at the center of the space displaying the unique melon-shaped vertical space. This is a device to add visual excitement and to encourage people to look up and down to other floors of shopping space.

The grand space of the atrium (4) and glass elevator is captured in the unique three-point perspective angle looking up toward the ceiling of the atrium space. This choice of viewpoint dramatically emphasizes and describes the space.

1

2

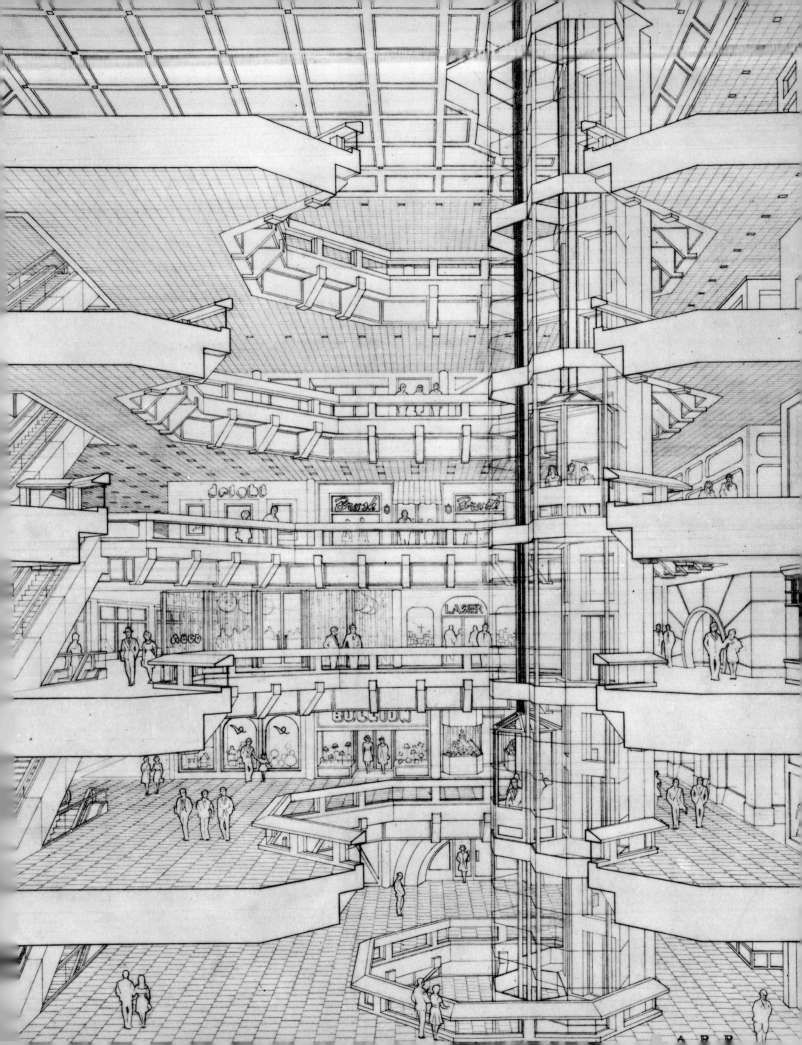

200

Airbrush

One of the most sophisticated techniques of all is the use of ink and airbrush.

Tesla has received many awards for his drawings, executed in black and white and in color. Most noticeable in his renderings are the subtle and sophisticated rendition of forms and the dramatic use of light.

In an airbrush drawing the ink-line work supplies the outline and architectural details of the building. After the drawing is completed in ink, the airbrush is used to supply tones and values to the sky and various parts of the building.

Tesla uses the three-point perspective whenever an aerial viewpoint is used and whenever the building exceeds a certain height above the observer. This dramatic use of perspective plus the skillful handling of light and shade is what separates these from the ordinary colored rendering.

Drawings by: Tesla

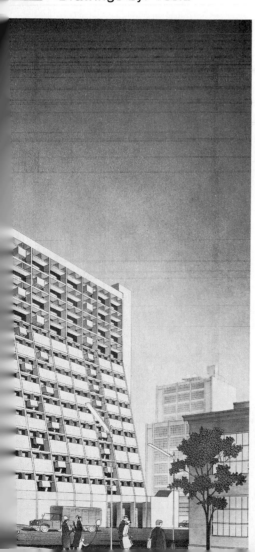

TESLA 1969

2

Aerial Superimposition

These two drawings are very different in style and demonstrate how the building dictates the technique. In an aerial superimposition, it is sometimes tempting to render the new project to look like the photograph. This can defeat the purpose, especially if the project is large. It will get lost in the cityscape.

Here the rendering was done in color and set into a black-and-white aerial photograph to make certain that the entire project was recognizable and distinguishable from the background (1). On other buildings where you are not concerned with the surroundings, you can have more freedom with your choice of medium. In this ground-level view (2), the choice was ink line and airbrush for the color tones.

Drawings by: Gregory Ihnatowicz

1

Photo Montage

This civic project is described by three different means. The first (1) is an aerial photograph that looks like the completed project. It is not. It is a model set into an existing aerial photo. The model was also used as a presentation tool and was further utilized as the basis for the layout of a ground-level perspective (2).

The aerial sketch (3) of a development at Crown Center reduces all surrounding elements to sketch form for a harmonious picture.

2

3

4

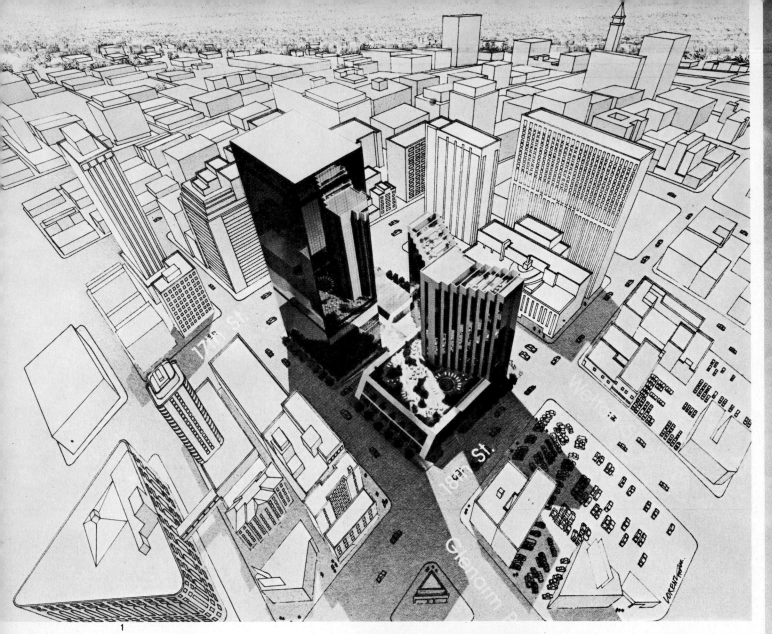

Photorendering

These two drawings were used in a promotional brochure. The first is an unusual aerial based on a "fish-eye" type of perspective (1), and the second is a rendered cutaway section. The sectional rendering is most unusual in that it was done separately in pen and ink and colored, then set into an enlarged color photograph (2) of a model of the project (3).

3

Drawings by: Albert Lorenz

Photodrawing

This rendering is pure photography. It combines three photographs into one composite. The site was a corner in Grand Central Station (1), which provided the major elements of the surroundings. But extra people were needed and Grand Central Station is an easy place to find them (2). The third element was obtained by photographing an 8x10 print of the façade at an angle similar to the perspective (3). The pictures were all cut out, assembled, and the edges retouched with black ink. Then this composite was rephotographed as the final product (4).

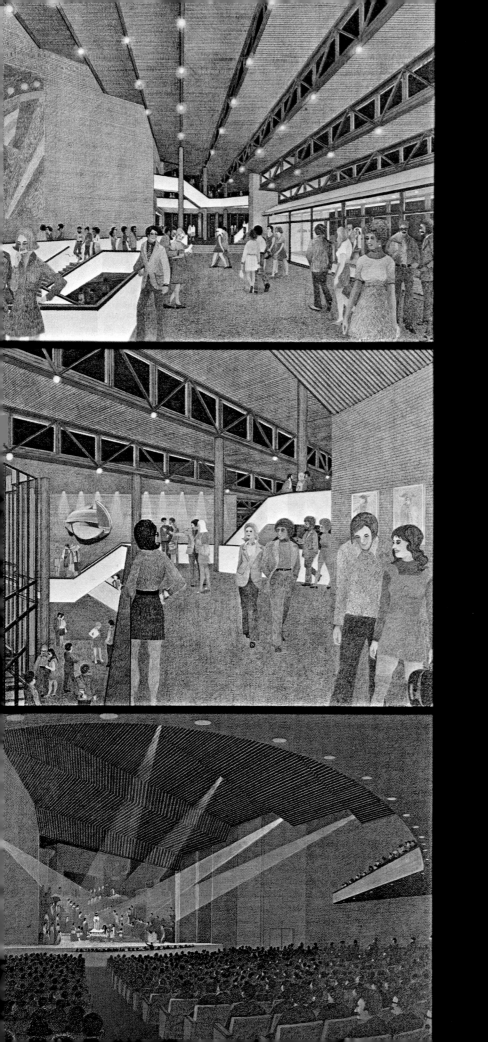

1

2

Coordinated Series

A coordinated series of drawings can have much more impact than a single view. However, there should be some element that holds the series together. In the theater drawings on pages 210–214, the unifying element was to show the building in use for a concert at evening time. Other unifying elements can be the close relationships of viewpoints, drawing techniques, and other stylistic devices. The unifying elements in the second project (6, 7) are the close relationships of forms and the soft-pencil drawing technique.

3   5

4

Cooper Union

These drawings were part of a fund-raising brochure and were all executed in the same drawing style and color technique. The layouts for some of these drawings can be seen on pages 76–77. A technique was developed using colored pencils on rough white illustration board where the figures were drawn without outlines. All the separations of form were done through placing value against value rather than with outlines.

Artwork, sculpture, and paintings were exact copies of real works, and the figures were developed from photographs of the students in action. The simple building forms and spaces became a backdrop for the color and activity of the figures.

Drawings by: Ernest Burden

4

6

The hilly character of San Francisco is captured in this series of ink-on-mylar sketches. The surroundings were done from photographs and the new structures rendered as part of the whole scene. The technique of vignette is used extensively in this series. It helps to focus attention on the project as well as to provide an interesting composition.

Drawings by: Walter Thomason

Telegraph Hill
Apartments

The Galleria

This series of drawings was intended to highlight the interior lobby space of a combination office-residential tower. The drawings were done in pen-and-ink line over and the tones were colored pencil. The exterior (1) showed the entire tower. A close-up of the entrance to the atrium lobby (2) showed the space beyond. The dramatic interior illustrated the multilayered space (3), yet kept the focus on the ground level by showing the colorful activity of the figures.

Drawings by: Brian Burr

Drawings by: Bob Watel

A delicate style for pen and ink makes this series of a bank building distinctive. Even though the surfaces are all rendered, there is an openness to the style.

Each of the drawings shows a different aspect of the building, yet each retains an overall recognition of the main building elements. The aerial focuses attention on the major drive-in courtyard. Other ground-level views have a similar focus on part of the courtyard and utilize the flags as one element of continuity. The extreme close-up is a detail of the gateway entrance.

Federal Reserve Bank

1

Yardarm

These drawings were produced primarily for a promotional brochure and for presentation of the design of a resort condominium on eastern Long Island.

The style chosen was a colored-marker undertone on rough illustration board. Rather than use a sand-colored board to relate to the beach tone, a white one was chosen so that the colors of the sky and water would not be altered by a colored board. Colored pencils were used over the magic-marker undercoat to build up the tones. In the beach drawings (1, 2), all the forms were defined by tones rather than outlines. The figures in the interior and balcony views were drawn with outlines to attract more attention to them as the center of focus (3, 4). Finally, in the room interior, a nighttime setting was preferred, with emphasis on more formal clothing.

2   4

Drawings by: Ernest Burden

3

1

2

3   4

Ten-Eyck Block

Pencil is the medium with the most versatility, especially when trying to draw traditional or classical forms of architecture. Round forms are easier to draw and shading is also more effective when using pencil. In this series, the main domed element appears in each of the views, making it easier to comprehend the relationship of each view.

Drawings by: Brian Burr

Retail Center

A good demonstration of the line drawing versus the value drawing can be seen in this series of a major shopping-center complex. One device Ron Love used often in open spaces like this one is the hanging vertical banners. They help to provide depth to the space and interest to the composition. It is often best to get a good ink-line drawing prior to a color version. For magazines, it will reproduce most clearly, even at a reduced scale.

Drawings by: Ron Love

3   4

1

Resort Hotel

Lush tropical vegetation and a resort atmosphere place this hotel near Rio de Janeiro. The pure ink-line style is used for all elements of the drawing, including the reflection in the water and the rendition of clouds in the sky.

2

Drawings by: Bob and Anna Fisher

1

Hunter College

Destined for a busy corner in Manhattan's Upper Eastside, this project was drawn to show one of the important elements of the project, the interconnecting pedestrian bridges (1). First, one view was drawn looking from the bridge into the corner courtyard (2), and then another showed the bridge as seen from inside the building (3). Another view was taken from an outside plaza with the bridge beyond (4), and finally a view from below showed the relationship to the busy street activity. The technique used was pure ink line, building up tones through ruled lines for the structure and free-hand texture for the shading of the figures.

Drawings by: Brian Burr

2

3

4

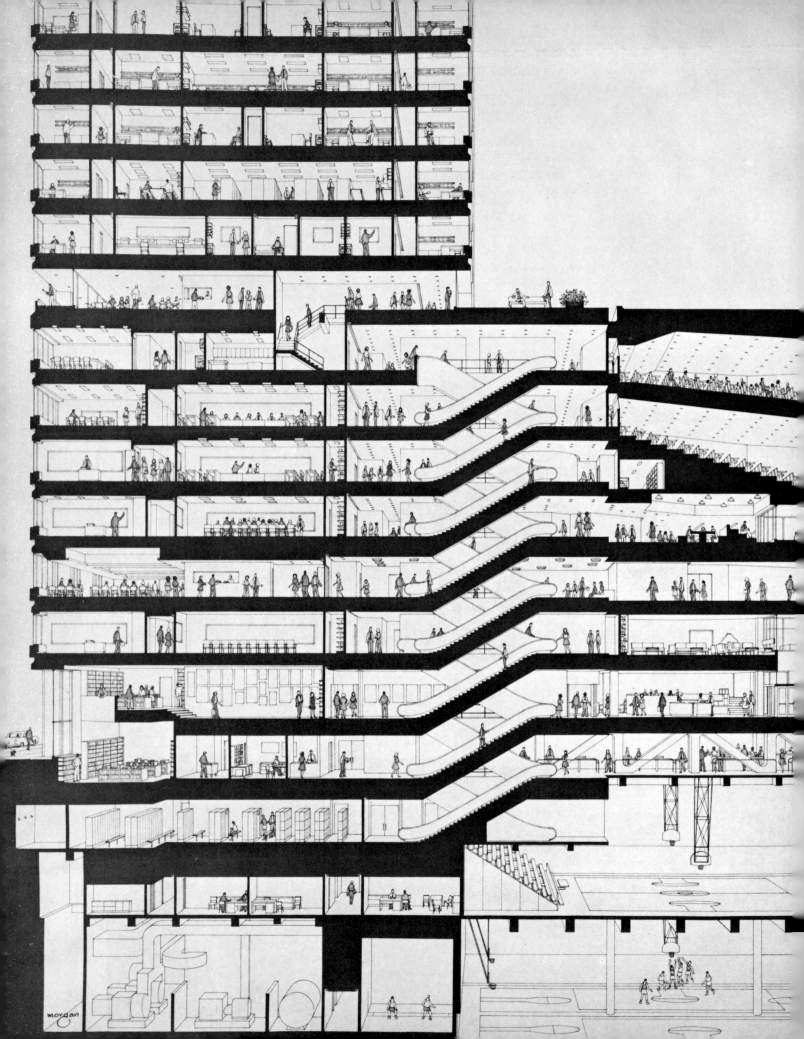

Hunter College

What Brian Burr did not show on the previous page is illustrated here in this cross section through the base of the new structure. Visible on the right side is the interconnecting bridge and the corner courtyard.

The scaled figures and furniture make this sectional drawing very realistic and descriptive of the complex of spaces within. By placing the eye level on the street level, areas below the street could be shown. To minimize distortion in the upper floors, furniture and figures are placed close to the edge of the cut section.

Drawing by: Dave Morgan

1

Office and Retail Complex

A strong watercolor technique and the choice of view contribute to this successful series. The close-in, low-level aerial describes the project (3), and each view has recognizable elements to relate it to the other drawings (1, 2). Finally, two interior views conclude the sequence (4, 5). The mountains in the background are recalled again in the view from inside one of the offices (4).

Drawings by: Ron Love

2   3

4

5

Urban Community

In the rendition of an entire new urban town, coordination is especially important. It was achieved here by several devices. Certain recognizable buildings show up in the background of each drawing. On the ground level, the amount of landscaping and the style of drawing the trees, figures, and cloud formations both contribute continuity. The crisp ink-line drawings were used for reproduction, and then colored versions were made for presentation.

Drawings by: Bob and Anna Fisher

4

5

Riverside Projects

In the drawing of the marina (2), buildings are used primarily as a backdrop with the main attention centered on the sailboats, flag, and activity on the pier. A view of the pier shows many items of entourage used to create the marina atmosphere.

In the riverfront drawing (3), structures are again treated as background elements, with the focus placed on the boardwalk activity. Here the elements of entourage are changed slightly to include cyclists and a group of figures flying a kite, as well as the tugboat on the river.

Without this appropriate use of entourage neither drawing would have quite the appeal it now has.

Drawings by: Mark deNalovy-Rozvadovski

Lawrence Hall of Science

This series of drawings, executed in pen and ink, was produced for entry in an architectural competition. Plans, elevations, sections, and perspectives were all related by technique.

Included in the presentation were two exterior perspectives. The basis for both perspective drawings was an aerial photograph of the entire area. It was decided to render them in that same overall format rather than enlarge the actual project area to a more standardized size.

Thus, each drawing had to make use of certain compositional devices to emphasize the actual project. Main arterial roads provided the compositional element in the aerial. Certain dominant and recognizable features of the university campus were emphasized to provide a unifying element within the series of drawings.

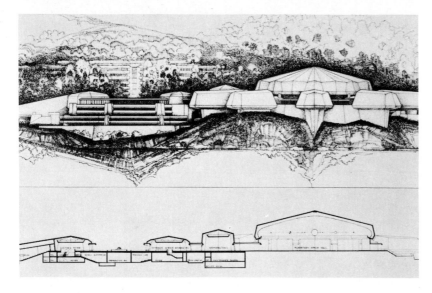

Lawrence Hall of Science

Private Residence

A simplicity of line and tone characterizes this series. A stylistic approach rather than a realistic representation of the trees and surroundings gives the drawings a graphic simplicity. This is combined with the use of vignette to create an impression by understatement.

Drawings by:
Remmert W. Huygens

1

2

3

4

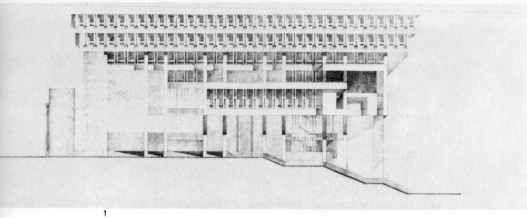

1

Boston City Hall

Many presentation drawings of this major project were published when it was the winner of a major design competition. This series, done in the architect's office, shows design studies through a sketch technique using pencil. The first sketch is an exterior elevation (1) followed by a sectional perspective (2). The third sketch is a view of the main stair entry. The final sketch is a rendered elevation.

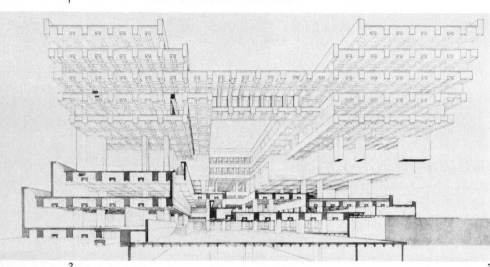

2

3

Drawings by:
Noel M. McKinnell

4

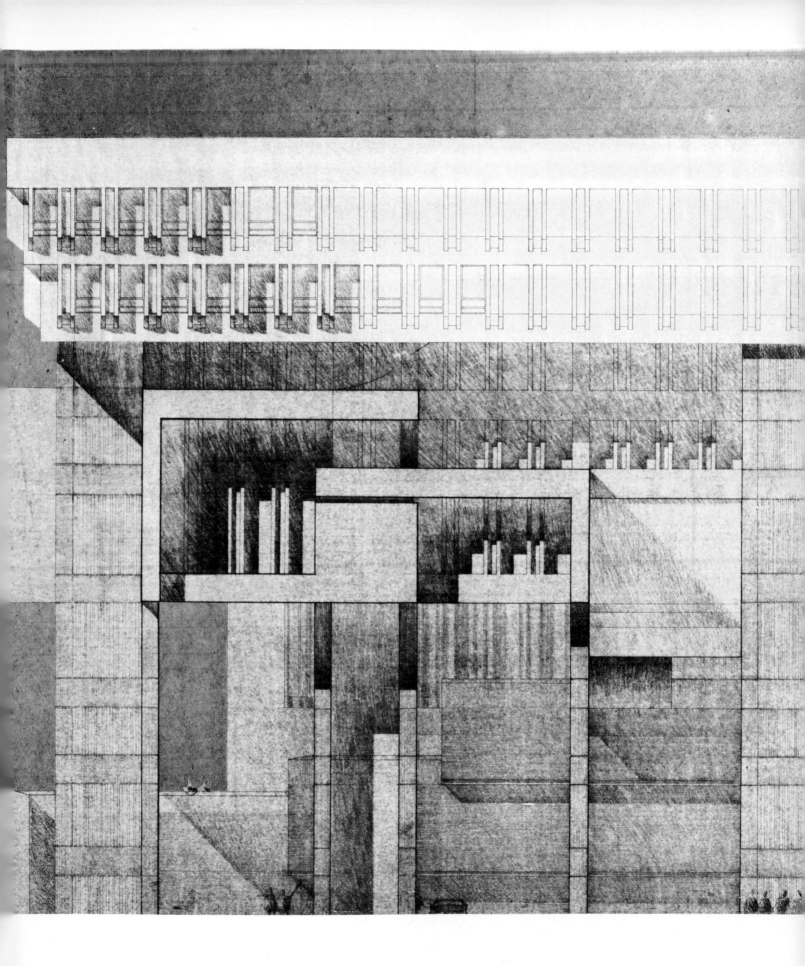

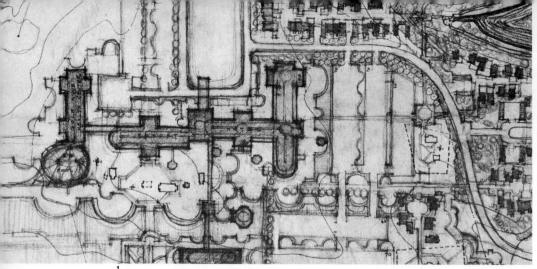

1

Kingsmill Center

Architects' study sketches are nearly always done in pencil, as it is a medium that can be altered easily as the drawings are developed. In this series, there is a continuity of style from the overall site plan (1) to the aerial perspective (5). The informal drawing style is appropriate to the architectural forms (2, 3, 4) and expresses their character more than a hard-line drawing.

Drawings by: James Bischoff

2

3

A RESORT HOTEL & CONFERENCE CENTER
KINGSMILL, VIRGINIA

4

5

1

2

Citicorp

Many drawings have been published of the Citicorp Building in Manhattan. But an integral part of the complex and an important aspect of the total development is St. Peter's Church, which occupies one corner of the site. The exterior facing the street is solid. Above it hovers the 50-story Citicorp Tower (1). Inside the tower is the multilevel atrium space (2), which houses commercial shops and restaurants.

The church has its own entry, and this series of drawings captures the drama of the angular interior space. The technique is simple pencil-line work with texture added by drawing over a rough board, as in stone rubbing. This technique allowed for an interesting play of light and shadow within the dramatic interior space (4, 5).

Drawings by: George Conley

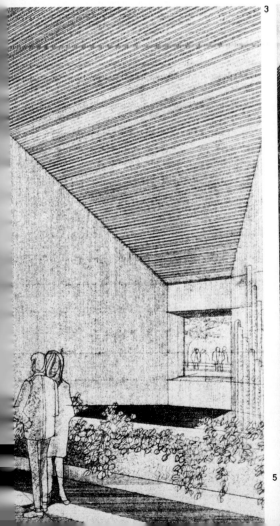

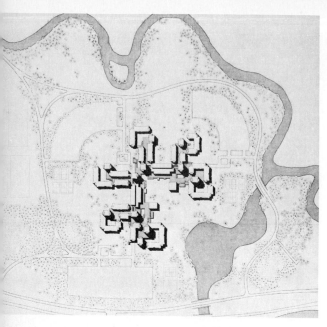

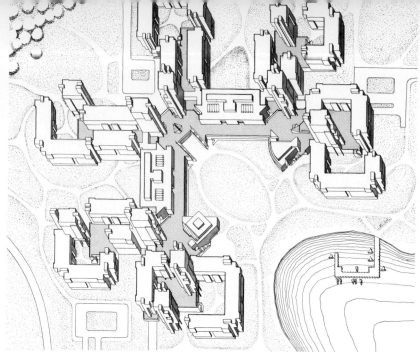

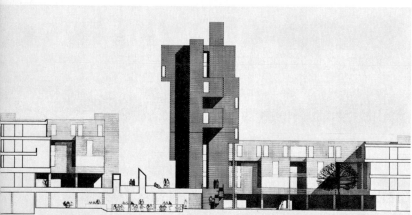

SUNY Dormitories

A plan of a building reveals only its location on the site. An axonometric perspective begins to explain the form but in a two-dimensional way. An elevation starts to depict the building as a reality. The overall perspective, even though it is only from one viewpoint, tells the most. Combined elevation and sections are very descriptive in showing the relationship of exterior to interior space. But the most descriptive is the close-up perspective sketch, done here with a free-hand ink line over a prepared mechanical layout.

Drawings by: Albert Bergman

Snowbird

The winter scene chosen for this series makes use of the snow-covered mountains as a design element. Rather than have the vast landscape and mountainous background obscure and overshadow the buildings, the architects achieved quite the opposite effect. Evergreen trees became design elements punctuating the landscape. The white space of the mountain backdrop was perfect for directing attention to the crisp detail on the structures. The final view at grade shows wintertime activity with the snow-covered mountains in the distance.

Drawings by: Franklin Ferguson

Urban Revitalization

Planner Charles Blessing is at home with any scale project and a pen. He can just as easily sketch an aerial view of half a city or half a city block. The style is straightforward. He draws only the essential features. He builds up tonal values along the major avenues of development and keeps control of the composition (3).

In the drawing for the renovation of an urban block in Detroit (1, 2), he captured the essence of the Victorian style with just a few simple lines depicting the ornate forms. The new structures are also added in a simple linear manner.

Drawings by: Charles Blessing

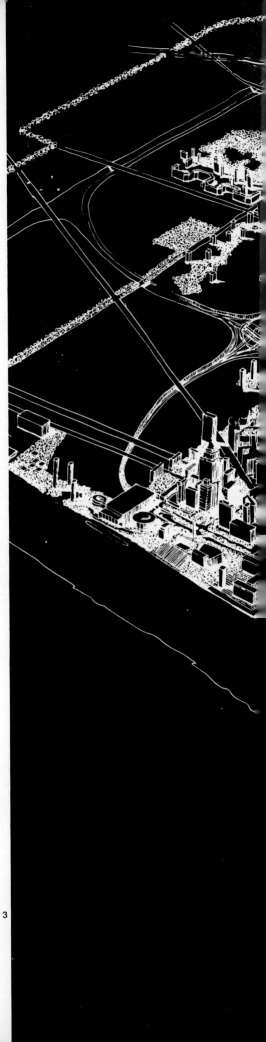

DESIGN CREDITS

16–18   5½ Way, PEDESTRIAN MALL
42d to 57th Streets, Between Fifth & Sixth Avenues, New York City
Pomerance & Breines, Architects, New York City

26–28   UNIVERSITY OF CALIFORNIA MEDICAL CENTER, San Francisco
Computer Plotted Perspectives
Anshen & Allen Architects, San Francisco

30–31   PROPOSED ELKS LODGE
Bakersfield, Calif.
Whitney Biggar, AIA, Architect
Bakersfield, Calif.
Ernest Burden, delineator

32–33   WEST HIGH SCHOOL
Kern High School District
Bakersfield, Calif.
Whitney Biggar, AIA, Architect
Ernest Burden, delineator

34–35   THE CUSTOM GRID
John F. Kennedy Senior High School
Sacramento, Calif.
Gordon Stafford, Architect
Sacramento, Calif.
Ernest Burden, delineator

36–37   VANDEN HIGH SCHOOL, Travis AFB, Calif.
VBN Corporation, Architects
Berkeley, Calif.
Ernest Burden, delineator

38–39   CAMELBACK INN, Scottsdale, Ariz.
Wm. Kenneth Frizzell, New York City
Flatow Moore Bryan and Associates, Phoenix, Ariz.
Ernest Burden, delineator

40–41   CAMELBACK INN—2
Wm. Kenneth Frizzell, New York City
Flatow Moore Bryan and Associates, Phoenix, Ariz.
Ernest Burden, delineator

42–43   LAKE DEVELOPMENT, Offenberg, West Germany
Retirement Complex, Luxury Apartments, Hotel and
Convention Center, and Beach Club
Abraham W. Geller & Associates
Architects and Planners, New York City
Ernest Burden, delineator

44–45   TEACHERS TRAINING UNIVERSITY
Heserak, Iran
Layout by Ernest Burden
Drawing by Robert Fisher

48–49   ROSEWOOD ESTATES (Proposed retirement home)
Bakersfield, Calif.
Whitney Biggar, AIA, Architect
Bakersfield, Calif.
Ernest Burden, delineator

50   SAN FRANCISCO FIREHOUSE
George T. Rockrise & Associates
Architects, Urban Designers, Land Planners
San Francisco
Ernest Burden, delineator

51   BERKELEY FIREHOUSE, Calif.
MBT ASSOCIATES, San Francisco
Ernest Burden, delineator

52–53   CIVIC AUDITORIUM, Redding, Calif.
VBN Corporation, Architects
Berkeley, Calif.
Ernest Burden, delineator

54–55   IBM CAFETERIA, Burlington, Vt.
Curtis & Davis, New York City
Ernest Burden, delineator

56–57   AMERICAN NATIONAL BANK, St. Paul, Minn.
The Eggers Group, P.C.
New York City
Ernest Burden, delineator

58–59   NEWARK GATEWAY Development, Newark, N.J.
60–61   Gruen Associates, New York City
Ernest Burden, delineator

62–63   BUNKER HILL APARTMENTS, Los Angeles
Robert E. Alexander, FAIA
Los Angeles
Ernest Burden, delineator

64   STANFORD SQUARE, Palo Alto, Calif.
Gerald Gamlier Weisbach, AIA, Architect
San Francisco
Ernest Burden, delineator

66–69   FOLEY SQUARE, New York City
Gruzen & Partners, Architects
New York City
Ernest Burden, delineator

70–71   MURRY BERGTRAUM HIGH SCHOOL FOR BUSINESS CAREERS
New York City
Gruzen & Partners, Architects, New York City
Ernest Burden, delineator

72–73   5TH & MISSION GARAGE, San Francisco
H. J. Degenkolb Associates, Engineers
San Francisco
Ernest Burden, delineator

74–75   BERKELEY HIGH SCHOOL CAFETERIA, Calif.
Corlett & Spackman, Architects
San Francisco
Ernest Burden, delineator

76–77   THE COOPER UNION FOUNDATION BUILDING
New York City
John Hejduk, Architect, New York City
Ernest Burden, delineator

78–79   PACIFIC TELEPHONE & TELEGRAPH CO.
Sacramento, Calif.
Dreyfus & Blackford, Architects
Sacramento, Calif.
Ernest Burden, delineator

80–81   ETCHEVERRY HALL, Step 2, University of California, Berkeley
Skidmore, Owings & Merrill, San Francisco
Ernest Burden, delineator

82–83   KAISER HOSPITAL ADDITION
Oakland, Calif.
Kaiser Engineers, Oakland, Calif.
Ernest Burden, delineator

203 OFFICE BUILDING, Fisher Brothers, Houston, Tex.
S.O.M., Architects, Chicago
Gregory Ihnatowicz, delineator

204 HARRY S. TRUMAN STATE OFFICE BUILDING
Jefferson City, Miss.
Patty Berkebile Nelson Duncan Monroe
Lefebvre Architects Planners Inc.
Kansas City
Julian Ominski, delineator

205 HYATT REGENCY AT CROWN CENTER, Kansas City
Patty Berkebile Nelson Duncan Monroe
Lefebvre Architects Planners, Inc.
Kansas City
Dick Sneary, delineator

206-207 DENVER SQUARE
S.O.M., Architects, Chicago
Al Lorenz, delineator

208 BOWERY SAVINGS BANK, Grand Central Station, New York City
Hellmuth, Obata & Kassabaum, New York City
Ernest Burden, delineator

210-212 AARON DAVIS HALL
The Leonard Davis Center for the Performing Arts
City College of New York
Abraham W. Geller & Associates
Ezra D. Ehrenkrantz and Associates
New York City
Ernest Burden, delineator

213 GOVERNMENT CENTER, Tanzania, A competition
Bond Ryder Associates Architects
New York City
Ernest Burden, delineator

214-215 THE COOPER UNION FOUNDATION BUILDING, New York City
John Hejduk Architect, New York City
Ernest Burden, delineator

216-217 TELEGRAPH HILL CONDOMINIUM, San Francisco
Backen, Arrignoi & Ross, Architects
San Francisco
Walter Thomason & Associates, delineator

218-219 THE GALLERIA, New York City
David Kenneth Specter Architect, New York City
Brian Burr, delineator

220-221 FEDERAL RESERVE BANK, Baltimore
Hellmuth, Obata & Kassabaum
St. Louis, Mo.
Robert G. Watel, Jr., delineator

222-223 YARDARM BEACH CONDOMINIUM, Westhampton, N.Y.
David Kenneth Specter, Architect
New York City
Ernest Burden, delineator

224-225 TEN EYCK BLOCKS, Albany, N.Y.
Gruen Associates Architects
New York City
Brian Burr, delineator

226-227 NEIMAN-MARCUS GALLERIE, Washington, D.C.
John Carl Warnecke, FAIA, Architects
Washington, D.C.
Ron Love, delineator

228-229 GUARUJA HOTEL, São Paulo, Brazil
Perkins & Will Architects
New York City
Bob and Anna Fisher, delineators

230 HUNTER COLLEGE, Office and Classroom Building, New York City
Ulrich Franzen Architects, New York City
Brian Burr, delineator

232-233 HUNTER COLLEGE, Office and Classroom Building, New York City
Ulrich Franzen Architects, New York City
Brian Burr, delineator

234-235 OFFICE-RETAIL COMPLEX, Vancouver, Canada
Waisman Associates Architects, Vancouver, Canada
Ron Love, delineator

236-237 PROJECT GLEBA "D", Barra Da Tijuca, Rio de Janeiro, Brazil
Slomo Wenkert Arquitetura y Planejamento Urbano Ltda.
Rio de Janeiro, Brazil
Bob and Anna Fisher, delineators

238-239 RIVERSIDE PROJECTS, Bellvue Environs, New York City
Davis Brody and Associates, Architects
New York City
Mark de Nalovy Rozvadovski, delineator

240-244 LAWRENCE HALL OF SCIENCE
University of California, Berkeley
Anshen & Allen, Architects
San Francisco
Ernest Burden, delineator

246 FOX HILLS BUSINESS PARK, Culver City, Calif.
Langdon & Wilson, Architects, Los Angeles
Robert Jackson, delineator

247 THE J. PAUL GETTY MUSEUM, Malibu, Calif.
Langdon & Wilson, Architects, Los Angeles
David F. Wilkins, delineator

248-249 FANEUIL HALL, Boston
Benjamin Thompson & Associates
Cambridge, Mass.
Carlos Diniz, delineator

250-251 PRIVATE RESIDENCE, Providence, R.I.
Huygens and DiMella, Inc. Architects, Boston
Remmert W. Huygens, delineator

252 BOSTON CITY HALL, Boston
Kallmann McKinnell & Knowles, Architects, Boston
Michael McKinnell, delineator

254-255 KINGSMILL HOTEL AND CONFERENCE CENTER
Kingsmill, Va.
Callister Payne & Bischoff
Tiburon, Calif.
1,2,3 James Bischoff, delineator
4,5 Terry Stephens, delineator

256-257 SAINT PETER'S CHURCH, Citicorp Center, New York City
Hugh Stubbins and Associates, Inc. Architects, Boston
George Conley, delineator

258-259 S.U.N.Y., Buffalo, N.Y.
Academic core and dormitories
David Brody & Associates, Architects
New York City
Albert Bergman, delineator

260-261 RESTON, Va.
Conklin & Rossant Architects, New York City
James Rossant, delineator

262 GERMANTOWN PROJECT
Conklin & Rossant Architects, New York City
James Rossant, delineator

263 RESTON, Va.
Conklin & Rossant Architects
James Rossant, delineator

264-265 SNOWBIRD RESORT, Utah
Brixen & Christopher Architects
Salt Lake City, Utah
Franklin Ferguson, delineator

VANISHING POINT;
1) A POINT AT WHICH A GROUP OF
RECEDING PARALLEL LINES SEEM
TO MEET WHEN REPRESENTING IN
LINEAR PERSPECTIVE 2) A POINT
AT WHICH SOMETHING DISAPEARS
OR CEASES TO EXIST